AIR FRYER COOKB(
BEGINNERS

A TRULY HEALTHY, OIL-FREE APPROACH TO LIFE & FOOD WITH 1000 DAYS OF BUDGET-FRIENDLY & EASY-BREEZY AIR FRYER RECIPES FOR THE WHOLE FAMILY

RACHEL VITALE

Rachel Vitale

Table of Contents

A Gift for You!!!

Hello and thank you for purchasing the book!

I have prepared a **NICE SURPRISE FOR YOU.** Scan the qr-code

NOW and find out how what *it's all about*!

2 EXTRA BONUS INSIDE

A Special Request

Your brief amazon review could really help us.

You know, this is very easy to do, go to the ORDERS section of your Amazon account and click on the "Write a review for the product" button. It will automatically take you to the review section.

INTRODUCTION

An air fryer is a kitchen appliance that converts air into heat to cook food. It circulates heated air around the food, causing moisture to evaporate and creating a crispy outer crust. Air fryers work best when the surrounding air is dry and above room temperature. Moist air will cause food to steam and lose its crispiness and flavor so that it ends up tasting like bland fried food.

Air frying cooks foods faster than conventional baking, boiling, or roasting methods. The crispy outside makes it an excellent way of cooking chips, roast potatoes, and many other potato side dishes without deep-frying them in oil.

The air fryer uses the same principle as convection ovens, where hot air is released in one direction and rises to the upper level. In this case, the hot air is circulated inside a sealed container (typically a perforated sealed bag or tube), and heated food is placed inside it. The hot air prevents contamination of food while it cooks. The air fryer uses a blower fan to pump heated air into the container. This heats the food to an internal temperature up to 400°F (200°C), enough to cook the food quickly and evenly.

The first air fryer was invented in 1987 by a French pastry chef to cook potatoes quickly. In 2008, the first air fryer was designed for home use and was produced on an assembly line in China.

There are several different air fryer models on the market today. Each features a different amount of internal volume. Larger air fryers are much more efficient because they have larger air filters and can cook more food at once.

There is a great variety in air fryers' designs; some models do not require preheating time. Models with preheat time may use up more energy. Some models of air fryers have a rotisserie attachment to cook meat and poultry, fish, and other foods with a crispy texture around the outside and tender on the inside. Many models use convection for cooking, which reduces cooking time by about 30% compared to conventional ovens and reduces fat intake by about 10%.

Cooking efficiencies vary depending on the container size and how often the contents should be emptied. The longevity of an air fryer varies depending on the model and can be affected by several factors.

The most common reason for replacing an air fryer is if it malfunctions, has a damaged motor, or has parts that have lost their effectiveness. Another reason could be that food gets clogged and creates a mess, preventing the appliance from completing its function. Suppose a deep fryer has been used for an extended period. In that case, the heating element may begin to malfunction or weaken.

1. The Features of an Air Fryer

Different brands of air fryers out there will have some "flair" of their own! However, the following features are common staples of every air fryer.

In general, an air fryer consists of:

1. **The Cooking Chamber:** The main body of the appliance that holds the food. It consists of a basket or wire rack to support the foods during cooking and a lid to contain the hot air around your food.

2. **The Handle:** A handle on the cooking chamber to take out your foods without burning your hands. The Handle is usually covered in a silicone sleeve for added grip and protection.

3. **The Power Cord:** This cord may be removable so that you have more freedom on where you can place your air fryer. Usually, the power cord is a standard/longer cable plugged into the wall.

4. **The Temperature Settings:** A digital display will show you your cooking parameters and other settings. The settings include setting the temperature for frying, sautéing, searing and baking. Some air fryers have preheated options so that you can let your air fryer get to the desired temperature before putting your foods in it.

5. **The Timer Control Knob:** This is to set the desired cook time. Some air fryers don't come with a timer, but this is not a feature that I think should be missing from an air fryer.

6. **The Lid:** The top of your air fryer. It is designed to seal the hot air and keep it circulating in your food.

7. **The Safety Switches:** All good-quality air fryers will have multiple layers of safety to ensure that you can use them safely. These layers all have one purpose. They all ensure you will be protected from getting burned by your air fryer. Air fryers also have other safety features such as child safety, auto-shutoff, overheating, etc.

8. **The Air Inlet:** The hole that gets a blast of hot air for the cooking process.

9. **The Air Outlet:** This outlet is usually perforated to allow for excess hot air to release from the cooking chamber.

As you can see, every one of these features has a specific purpose. While these are the typical features of an air fryer, not all air fryers will necessarily have these features.

One of the main reasons why some air fryers don't include certain features is because it might be cost-ineffective to put those extra features into them. Also, it's natural for a company to put more cost and energy into making their device more powerful and efficient than adding functionality that may not be necessary. In the end, it's the features that are important when choosing the right model of the air fryer.

2. Benefits of Air Fryer

The air fryer is a device you can use on your countertops. It looks like a vase, but it has a heating element in the base that circulates hot air around food for cooking. Here are many benefits of using an air fryer: cooking very quickly and evenly, there is no need to add any oil, it saves you money by saving you time and dishes to wash, and because of such a light frying process, frozen foods are not going to lose nutrients.

Here are the major benefits of using an air fryer.

It is a healthy and green cooking device. The air fryer uses less fat and doesn't need oil to cook; you can use your favorite oil without the danger of having a heart attack after eating it in no time. It's very easy to clean, and it saves time as well. The air fryer comes in different sizes, so you can use it for baking and grilling food simultaneously.

The air fryer is not the same as your regular oven; it uses a different technology based on circulating hot air rather than cooking with heat. There are different cooking modes, such as convection and non-convection. The non-convection mode helps to cook the food faster, but it also cooks unevenly due to heat fluctuations in the oven causing moisture loss.

The convection mode is recommended if you want your food to be cooked evenly and quickly. When using this mode, the oil and the food are cooked with alternating heat, heated faster in a certain area, and then dropped to a place for cooling. This helps cook evenly and quickly because it maintains the proper temperature throughout the device.

The air fryer can cook frozen foods without compromising nutrients in the process. Depending on the meal's quantity and the cooking method, the cooking time might vary greatly. As such, it's best to use a meat thermometer when cooking because of the different thicknesses of food. Otherwise, you risk leaving food raw inside while it is overcooked on the outside. A good tip to try air frying with frozen foods is to cut them into small pieces before putting them into your air fryer.

The air fryer is safe as well. The inside is lined with a non-stick coating that reduces the risk of the oil spattering out. Also, it features a cool-touch handle and a safety interlock system to help prevent food from getting stuck into the heating element. Aside from that, the air fryer also helps keep your kitchen clean. It doesn't require much maintenance or cleaning because all you have to do is wipe it off with a towel after every use.

3. Tips and Tricks for the Air Fryer

If you're health-conscious, you may want to consider an air fryer as a healthy alternative to deep-frying. While that can take up space, it is worth the investment because it is easy to clean and use little oil.

1. **Don't fill the basket all the way:** If you're making a snack with many pieces, you can fill it halfway instead of filling it up. This allows the oil to circulate better and makes sure that everything gets cooked evenly. You can always add more pieces to fill the basket if you find it is not filled enough to cook them evenly.

2. **Don't let the oil get too hot:** Oil that is too hot will not be able to circulate properly. It will pool at the bottom, coating everything on its way to the basket. So, ensure that the oil is not too hot, which can happen quickly if you prepare a large amount of food. You can check how much your oil is heated by placing a few drops in the basket. If it

sizzles and bubbles, you need to turn down the heat or add more cold water if you want to reduce it.

3. **Use the right temperature and time:** When preparing food using an air fryer, there are many models, most of which cook at different temperatures. If you are unfamiliar with each one, check the instructions for using it correctly before you start cooking. The recommended temperature will depend on what you're cooking. Use a lower temperature if you are cooking something with many liquids, such as chicken wings, to prevent the oil from popping or boiling.

4. **Use a thermometer:** To ensure that your food is cooked properly and fully, use a thermometer. If you don't have one, most air fryers come with built-in thermometers to set the temperature and time before leaving it alone to cook. Ensure the temperature is not higher than recommended, and the device beeps when your food is ready to serve.

5. **Cook small portions:** You may want to consider cooking much food in one batch, but this will prevent your oil from circulating properly. It'll stick to the bottom of the basket with every other piece of food you add, making it harder for them to cook properly. Instead, try to stick to small batches so that you can ensure the best results for your food.

6. **Use precision cooking:** Precision cooking is a great way to ensure that whatever you're cooking comes out perfectly every time. This allows you to set the temperature on a timer, giving you total control over your food and ensuring it cooks properly. This setting is great for cooking food so you can clean up the air fryer before bed. If you find that your food is not done cooking when the timer goes off, you can restart the timer, and your air fryer will remember what temperature it was set at.

7. **Use a non-stick pan or mat:** This ensures your food doesn't stick to the bottom of the basket or pan. It also helps with cleaning if some bits get stuck in your pan. Using the non-stick mat properly takes much practice, so you aren't always cleaning it up, but it's worth the effort. If you do not have any, you can use parchment paper or pieces of foil to make sure your basket doesn't stick to the bottom too much.

8. **Check the basket frequently:** You will want to check it often while cooking most foods. When you're cooking something that you want to get crispy, you'll want to turn the food halfway through cooking to avoid overcooking and dryness. You can also check your ingredients to see if they need more of a particular ingredient, such as chicken wings or asparagus may need more oil than what is already in the basket. You can even stir and shake the basket while it's cooking to ensure that the food cooks.

9. **Clean before use:** Always clean your air fryer before each use so that there is no build-up after cooking. Some brands even have removable baskets so you can easily clean them when you're done. You can also soak the basket in diluted bleach and scrub it with a sponge. Some air fryers even have brushes designed to make the basket easier to clean up because you'll get food stuck in it, which may not come out easily.

10. **Use a healthy oil:** You will want to use a healthy oil for your air fryer because it isn't as good for you if your food becomes rancid after being heated. You can also find different oils you can use, and there are even air fryers with built-in oils, so you don't need to purchase them separately.

4. How to Convert Recipes used in Oven to Air Fryer

Converting recipes used in the oven to the air fryer is a great way to reduce the fat and calories in your diet while ensuring that you enjoy tasty, home-cooked meals. Saving money on expensive fast food is possible because of the adjustments you can make to a recipe that uses an oven.

This cooking is a great alternative for those days when you are too tired or don't want to stand in front of a stove preparing and cooking everything yourself. To reduce the time you spend cooking meals, you can use your air fryer to cook a few different recipes at one time and then store them in the refrigerator for later.

It is easy to convert because it takes time and trial and error. Each oven cooks differently, so some recipes may bake even better in an air fryer that doesn't use as much heat.

To convert recipes used in the oven to the air fryer, some instructions say things like "bake at 375°F [190°C]," but that's too high for the amount of heat an air fryer generates. The recipe will only do well at 300°F [150°C]or lower. Place your air fryer basket in the appliance and note how high the basket is positioned.

Since most recipes are written for baking in an oven rather than an air fryer, all you need to do is figure out how long it will take for the food to cook at 300°F [150°C]or lower. You can easily time this by using a stopwatch, checking on your food after a certain amount, then increasing or decreasing that time when you make that recipe again.

Guidelines for Recipes Conversion:

1. Convert temperature and time
2. You will need to reduce the amount of fat in your recipe. Air fryers do not use as much fat for cooking the food like an oven, so you will need less than a recipe calls for when converting to an air fryer. Test your food before serving to see if it needs more or less fat.
3. You may need to reduce the time needed to cook in the air fryer because it doesn't take as long to cook as it would in an oven.
4. Many recipes will be air fried in just a few minutes, so watch your food carefully and remove it the second it meets your requirements.
5. Suppose you are following a recipe that uses seasonings or herbs. In that case, you will have to add them near the end because they will burn quickly in an air fryer and give your food a bitter taste.
6. For some recipes, you may need to increase the amount of salt added because an air fryer does not heat food as well as an oven, so you will lose more natural juices in your foods.
7. Even with all these adjustments, you will still use less fat and calories than if you cooked those same foods in a traditional oven.

8. You can experiment to find new ways to make air fryer recipes more delicious. If you have a healthy lifestyle, try experimenting with alternative ingredients and different cooking styles, such as grilling, steaming, and baking.

5. Food to Cook in Air Fryer and Food to Avoid

Many foods work well for cooking in an air fryer: French fries, chicken nuggets, and cookies.

Avoid foods that aren't cooked well in an air fryer is always a good idea. These include fresh fruits, vegetables, and other foods that take time to cook.

Other foods to avoid are the foods you shouldn't cook in an air fryer because they will end up as unappetizing curdles or soups. They include tofu, tempeh, sprouts, and beans.

A good general rule is to cook solid, sliceable foods a little thicker than fries. These include fish fillets, chicken breasts, pork chops, and steak.

Avoid foods that are not as solid or thick as these because they are not cooked well in the air fryer and absorb much oil. You may even stop using your air fryer if you don't watch it carefully.

Below are some foods that can be cooked in an air fryer and those which should be avoided.

- **Cakes and other baked goods:** cakes and other baked goods generally work very well in an air fryer. You can either bake them on wire racks or on paper towels.
  Be careful not to overlap the racks when placing them inside the air fryer. If you plan on baking more than one item at a time, such as a cake and some cookies, then place the cake on the rack closest to the heating element.
  If you want to bake something more fragile, like a flan, place it on the rack further away from the heating element. Since it cooks faster than normal baking methods, remember to check on your cake regularly. Your air fryer brand's maximum temperature should also not be exceeded while using your appliance.

- **Bagels:** bagels are a great item to make in an air fryer. Only you have to be very careful when preparing them.

  If you're making bagels, ensure they are thoroughly cooled before placing them in your air fryer. It is best to place the racks on top of a baking sheet to catch any drips or spills. Then place them in the air fryer and cook at 375°F [190°C] for 15 minutes.

  Check on the bagels after 10 minutes to make sure they are crisp and done. You'll know they are ready when you can easily insert a toothpick into them.

- **Biscuits:** biscuits cook very well in an air fryer once you get past the awkwardness of figuring out how to place them into the air fryer.

  First, start by placing them in a single layer on top of wire racks. Bake them on the middle rack of your air fryer. After 20 minutes, remove the trays and check your biscuits. They should be hard and well browned. If they aren't done yet, place them back in the oven until they are done to your liking.

  If you find that they are not browning as much as you want, you can adjust the temperature or ensure you don't overfill the tray with biscuits. It may take a few tries to master this, but once you do, you'll be able to make biscuits in your air fryer almost as quickly and easily as you'd normally make them in your oven.

- **Casseroles:** casseroles are great items to make in an air fryer. They cook faster than they would in an oven, so they are ready sooner.

  It is best to cover the top of the casserole with aluminum foil before placing it into the air fryer. Cook at 375°F [190°C] for 20 minutes. Place the tray in your refrigerator while preparing the rest of the meal.

  Refrigerate the casserole for 20-30 minutes before baking, then transfer it to a wire rack and finish baking at 400°F [200°C] for 20-30 minutes more.

- **Desserts:** desserts such as cakes, pies, cookies, and brownies can be baked in an air fryer with no problem whatsoever. But if you're making something a little more pasty or sheer, such as pudding, you have to be careful not to overfill the air fryer.

  You should also ensure that your air fryer is set to the right temperature. If your air fryer brand has digital temperature control, it should be pre-set to 375°F [190°C].

If you have an air fryer that doesn't have temperature control, then you should pre-heat the air fryer to 375°F [190°C] before making your dessert. Cook at 375°F [190°C] for 20 minutes. Then remove the tray from the air fryer, place it on a wire rack and bake at 400°F [200°C] for 15-30 minutes until done.

Just remember that it takes less time to cook and reheat in a microwave oven than in an air fryer.

- **Fish:** Fish is another food you can cook in your air fryer. It should be placed in a single layer on top of wire racks and then cooked at 375°F [190°C] for 20 minutes or until done.

- **Fresh fruits:** fresh fruits don't work well when cooked in an air fryer. However, you can use them except for bananas, which should be left under a closed plastic bag and then cooked at 375°F [190°C] for 20 minutes.

  After that time has expired, open the plastic bag and check on it to see whether they look cooked. If not, leave the fresh fruits in the air fryer for another 15 minutes or so until they turn to mush.

  You can also make a fruit salad in an air fryer, but it's best to make it ahead of time and then cover the dish with a plastic bag and place it in your refrigerator overnight so the flavors can mingle.

  Then proceed with the instructions for making fresh fruits by placing them on top of wire racks and cooking them at 375°F [190°C] for 20 minutes or until done.

- **Mushrooms:** mushrooms cook well in an air fryer but tend to become soft and rubbery. So, if you want to use the air fryer for cooking mushrooms, you'll need to cook them separately and add them to other dishes after they are cooked.

  Place the mushrooms on top of wire racks leaving at least a 1-inch [2,5 cm] gap between the mushrooms and the racks. Cook at 400°F [200°C] for 15 minutes.

  Then remove the tray from the air fryer, cover them with a towel and leave them to cool while you start cooking the rest of your dinner.

Cooking in an air fryer isn't just fast and easy and a great alternative to cooking in your oven. And while some people hesitate to try something new, they should remember that air fryers aren't that different from regular ovens. You must learn how to use it properly and cook it as you normally would in your oven or microwave. And most of all, have fun.

BREAKFAST

1. Air Fryer Frittata

Serves: 1

Prep Time: 5 minutes

Cooking Time: 10 minutes

Ingredients

- 1 tablespoon (15 gr) chopped red bell pepper
- 1 tablespoon (15 ml) ghee or melted butter
- 1 tablespoon (15 gr) green onions, chopped
- 1 tablespoon (15 ml) heart-healthy oil
- 2 large eggs, beaten
- Salt and pepper to taste

Directions:

1. Preheat the air fryer at 350°F/180°C for 5 minutes.
2. Combine all ingredients in a mixing bowl.
3. Pour the egg mixture into a greased cake pan that will fit in the air fryer.
4. Place the cake pan with the egg mixture in the air fryer.

5. Air fry at 350°F/180°C for 10 minutes. Serve and enjoy!

Nutritional Fact Per Serving: Calories: 374; Carbohydrates: 2 g; Protein: 13 g; Fat: 35 g; Sugar: 1 g; Sodium: 235 mg; Fibre: 0.3 g

2. Asparagus, Cheese, and Egg Strata

Servings: 4

Prep Time: 15 minutes

Cooking Time: 10 minutes

Ingredients:

- ½ cup (50 gr) grated Havarti or Swiss cheese
- 1 tbsp. (15 ml) water
- 2 slices whole-wheat bread, cut into ½-inch [1,5 cm] cubes
- 1 bunch of flat-leaf parsley, chopped
- 3 tbsp. (45 ml) whole milk
- 4 eggs
- 6 asparagus spears, cut into 2-inch pieces [5cm]
- Cooking spray

Direction:

1. Place a 6×6×2-inch/15x15x5 cm baking pan into the air fryer basket. Add one tbsp water and asparagus spears into the pan.
2. Put the air fryer lid on and cook in the preheated air fryer at 325°F/170°C for

3 to 5 minutes, or until the asparagus spears are tender.

3. Remove the asparagus spears from the baking pan. Drain and dry them thoroughly. Place the asparagus spears and bread cubes in the pan, then spray with cooking spray. Set aside.
4. Add the cheese, parsley, salt, and pepper.
5. Put the air fryer lid on and bake at 350°F/180°C for 11 to 14 minutes until a knife inserted at the centre comes out clean.
6. Remove the strata from the pan. Let cool for 5 minutes before serving.

Nutritional Fact Per Serving Calories: 1214 kcal Fat: 90.11g Carbs: 6.16g Protein: 32.73g

3. Bacon-Wrapped Avocado

Servings: 24

Preparation Time: 5 minutes

Cooking Time: 8 minutes

Ingredients

- 3 avocados
- 24 thin strips of bacon
- ¼ cup (50 ml) ranch dressing for serving

Directions:

1. Slice every avocado into eight wedges of equal size.

2. Wrap each wedge with a bacon strip and, if necessary, cut the bacon.
3. Working in batches, place a single layer in an air fryer basket.
4. Cook for 8 minutes at 400°F/200°C until the bacon is fried and crispy.
5. Serve warm with the ranch.

Nutritional Fact Per Serving: Calories: 120; Carbs: 3 g; Protein: 8.3 g; Fat: 23.3 g

3. Add the spinach and season with salt and pepper to taste.
4. Pour all ingredients into a greased baking dish that will fit in the air fryer.
5. Bake at 350°F/180°C for 15 minutes. Serve and enjoy!

Nutritional Fact Per Serving: Calories: 198; Carbohydrates: 3 g; Protein: 8.3 g; Fat: 23.3 g; Sugar: 0.4 g; Sodium: 136 mg; Fibre: 1.4 g

4. Baked Spinach Omelette

Servings: 4

Preparation Time: 5 minutes

Cooking Time: 15 minutes

Ingredients

- ¼ cup (50 ml) coconut milk
- 1 tbsp. (15 ml) melted butter
- 2 tbsp. (30 ml) olive oil
- 4 large eggs, beaten
- 8 ounces (225 gr) baby spinach, chopped finely
- Cooking spray
- Salt and pepper to taste

Directions:

1. Preheat the air fryer to 350°F/180°C for 5 minutes.
2. In a mixing bowl, combine the eggs, coconut milk, olive oil, and butter until well combined.

5. Blueberry Spelt Pancakes

Servings: 4

Prep Time: 10 minutes

Cooking Time: 10 minutes

Ingredients:

- 1 cup (250 ml) hemp milk
- 1/2 cup (175 gr) Agave
- 1/2 cup (100 gr) blueberries
- 1/2 cup (125 ml) spring water
- A pinch of Sea Moss
- 2 cups (300 gr) spelt flour
- 2 tbsp. (25 gr) grape seed
- 2 tbsp. (25 gr) Hemp Seeds
- Grape seed oil

Directions:

1. Place Moss, agave, hemp seeds, grape seed oil, and spelt in a large bowl and mix well.
2. Add milk and water, and mix until you have your desired

consistency. Toss in blueberries and toss well.

3. Preheat your air fryer to 325°F/170°C.

4. Transfer batter to air fryer basket lined with parchment paper.

5. Cook for 3-4 minutes, flip and cook for 3 minutes more until golden on both sides. Serve and enjoy!

Nutritional Fact Per Serving: Calories: 276 kcal Carbs: 36g Fat: 11g Protein: 9g

6. Breakfast Balls "The bomb."

Servings: 2

Prep time: 20 min

Cook time: 25 min

Ingredients:

- Bacon slices, center-cut (3 pieces)
- 1 tbsp. Chives, fresh, chopped (1 bunch)
- Cooking spray
- 1 oz. (25 gr) Cream cheese, 1/3-reduced-fat, softened
- Eggs, large, lightly beaten (3 pieces)
- 4 oz. (100 gr) Pizza dough, whole wheat, freshly prepared

Directions:

1. Cook the bacon ingredient over medium heat until crisp and browned. Crumble and set aside in a bowl.

2. Cook eggs in the bacon fat until almost set. Add eggs to the bowl filled with crumbled bacon. Stir along with the chives and cream cheese.

3. Cut pizza dough into four pieces, then roll to form 5-inch/13 cm rounds. Fill each dough round with egg mixture (1/4 portion). Brush water on the edges before wrapping and pinching into a purse.

4. Add dough purses into the air fryer to cook for five minutes at 350°F/180°C.

Nutritional Fact Per Serving: Calories 305 Fat 15.0 g Protein 19.0 g Carbohydrates 26.0 g

7. Breakfast Cheese Rolls

Servings: 2

Prep Time: 15 min

Cooking time: 10 min

Ingredients:

- 3/4 cup (80 gr) Cheddar cheese, shredded
- Eggs, beaten lightly (2 pieces)

- 3/4 cup (100 gr) Manioc starch
- 3/4 cup (100 gr) Manioc starch, sweet
- 1/4 cup (60 ml) Milk, whole
- 1/4 cup (60 ml) Olive oil, extra virgin
- 1/2 cup (50 gr) Parmigiano-Reggiano cheese, grated finely
- 1 tsp. Salt
- 1/4 cup (60 ml) Water

Directions:

1. Set the air fryer at 325°F/170°C to preheat.
2. Combine the sour manioc and sweet manioc starches.
3. Combine milk with salt, olive oil, and water, then heat until boiling. Lower heat before stirring in the starches. Keep stirring until you have an extremely dry mixture. Let cool.
4. Stir the eggs into the cooled starch mixture to form a smooth dough. Mix well with the Parmigiano-Reggiano and Cheddar cheeses before shaping into golf-ball-sized pieces.
5. Cook dough pieces in the parchment-lined air fryer for eight to ten minutes.

Nutritional Fact Per Serving: Calories 97 Fat 5.5 g Protein 2.7 g Carbohydrates 9.2 g

8. Breakfast Stuffed Peppers

Servings: 2

Prep Time: 10 min

Cooking time: 15 min

Ingredients:

- 4 eggs
- 1 tsp. olive oil
- 1 bell pepper halved
- A pinch of salt and pepper
- A pinch of sriracha flakes for spice

Directions:

1. Cut bell peppers in half lengthwise and remove seeds and middle leaving the edges intact like bowls.
2. Use your finger to rub a bit of olive oil just on the exposed edges (where it was cut).
3. Crack two eggs into bell pepper half and sprinkle with some desired spices.
4. Set them on a dish straight into the air fryer's basket and close the lid on your air fryer.
5. Turn the machine on, press the air crisper button at 390°F/200°C for 13 minutes (times will vary slightly according to how well you like your egg).
6. Alternatively, if you would rather have your bell pepper eggless

brown on the outside, add just one egg to your pepper and set the air fryer to 330°F/170°C for 15 minutes.

Nutritional Fact Per Serving: Calories 164 Fat 5.5 g Protein 2.7 g Carbs 9.2 g

9. Buttermilk Breakfast Biscuits

Servings: 4

Prep time: 10 minutes

Cooking time: 8 minutes

Ingredients:

- A pinch baking soda
- ½ cup (75 gr) self-rising flour
- ½ teaspoon baking powder
- 1 cup (200 gr) buttermilk
- 2 cup (300 gr) white flour
- 1 tbsp. (15 gr) melted butter
- 1 tsp. (5 gr) sugar
- 1/4 cup (50 gr) butter, cold and cubed
- Maple syrup for serving

Directions:

1. Mix white flour with self-rising flour, baking soda, baking powder, and sugar in a bowl and stir.
2. Add cold butter and stir using your hands. Add buttermilk, stir until you obtain a dough, and transfer to a floured working surface. Roll your dough and cut 10 pieces using a round cutter.
3. Arrange biscuits in your air fryer's cake pan, brush them with melted butter and cook at 400°F/200°C for 8 minutes.
4. Serve them for breakfast with some maple syrup on top. Enjoy!

Nutritional Fact Per Serving: calories 192, fat 6, fiber 9, carbs 12, protein 3

10. Candied Walnut and Strawberry

Servings: 4

Prep Time: 10 minutes

Cooking Time: 10 minutes

Ingredients:

- 1 tbsp. (15 ml) raw agave nectar
- 1/2 cup (100 gr) walnuts, chopped
- A pinch of salt

Dressing

- 2 tsp. (10 ml) lime juice
- 1 tsp. onion powder
- 1/2 cup (125 ml) grape seed oil
- 1/2 cup (125 gr) strawberries, sliced
- 1/2 tsp. ginger
- A pinch of dill
- A pinch of salt
- 2 tbsp. (10 gr) shallots

- 2 tsp. raw agave nectar

Directions:

1. Coat walnuts with agave and salt.
2. Transfer to a cooking basket lined with parchment.
3. Preheat your air fryer to 300°F/150°C, roast for 6-8 minutes, and let them cool. Add dressing ingredients to a bowl, and blend for half a minute.
4. Add walnuts. Mix and enjoy!

Nutritional Fact Per Serving: Calories: 260 kcal Carbs: 28g Fat: 16g Protein: 4g

11. Delicious Breakfast Soufflé

Servings: 4

Prep time: 10 minutes

Cooking time: 8 minutes

Ingredients:

- 2 tbsp. (1 bunch) of chives, chopped
- 2 tbsp. (1 bunch) of parsley, chopped
- 4 eggs, whisked
- 4 tbsp. (60 gr) heavy cream
- A pinch of red chili pepper, crushed
- Salt and black pepper to the taste

Directions:

1. Mix eggs with salt, pepper, heavy cream, red chili pepper, parsley, and chives in a bowl, stir well and divide into 4 soufflé dishes.
2. Arrange dishes in your air fryer and cook soufflés at 350°F/180°C for 8 minutes.
3. Once done, serve them hot and enjoy!

Nutrition: calories 300, fat 7, fibre 9, carbs 15, protein 6

12. Easy Hash Browns

Servings: 4

Prep Time: 15 min

Cooking time: 30 min

Ingredients:

- 1 tbsp. (15 ml) Olive oil, extra virgin
- Jalapeno, w/ seeds removed, sliced into one-inch rings (1 piece)
- 1 ½ pound (700 gr) Potatoes, peeled, sliced into one-inch (2,5 cm) chunks
- Onion, small, sliced into one-inch (2,5 cm) chunks (1 piece)
- Bell pepper, red, w/ seeds removed, sliced into one-inch portions (1 piece)
- 1/2 tsp. Seasoning mix, taco
- 1/2 tsp. Olive oil, extra virgin

- 1/2 tsp. Cumin, ground
- A pinch of Salt
- A pinch of Black pepper, freshly ground

Directions:

1. Let the potatoes sit in cold water for twenty minutes. Meanwhile, set the air fryer at 320°F/160°C to preheat.
2. Drain, pat dry, and coat the potatoes with olive oil. Cook in the air fryer for eighteen minutes.
3. Toss the onion, jalapeno, bell pepper with olive oil, ground cumin, pepper, salt, and taco seasoning.
4. Combine the air-fried potatoes with the veggie mixture. Place in your air fryer and cook at 365°F/180°C for ten minutes.

Nutritional Fact Per Serving: Calories 186 Fat 4.3 g Protein 4.0 g Carbohydrates 33.70 g

13. French Toast Sticks

Servings: 18 sticks

Prep Time: 60 minutes

Cooking Time: 6 minutes

Ingredients

- 2 tbsp. (30 gr) sugar
- 1 teaspoon vanilla extract
- ½ tsp. ground cinnamon
- 1 cup (100 gr) cornflakes, optional
- 6 slices day-old Texas toast
- 4 large eggs
- 1 cup (250 ml) whole milk
- Confectioners' sugar for serving, optional
- Maple syrup

Directions:

1. Slice each piece of bread into thirds and place in a 13x9-inch (30x20 cm) baking dish that has not been greased.
2. Mix the eggs, milk, sugar, vanilla, and cinnamon in a large mixing bowl.
3. Pour over the bread and soak for two minutes, turning halfway through. Coat the bread in cornflakes crumbs on all sides if desired.
4. Place in a 15x10x1-inch (40x25x3 cm) greased baking pan. Freeze for 45 minutes or until firm. Place in the freezer in an airtight container or a resealable freezer bag.
5. Preheat the air fryer to 350°F/180°C.
6. Place the desired number of cookies on a greased tray in the air-fryer basket. 3 minutes in the oven. Cook for another 2–3 minutes, or until golden brown.
7. If desired, sprinkle with confectioners' sugar. Serve with syrup.

Nutritional Fact Per Serving: Calories per sticks: 184; Carbs: 3.5 g; Protein: 5.1 g; Fat: 11.1 g

14.   Fried Quiche

Servings: 8

Prep Time: 10 minutes

Cooking Time: 20 minutes

Ingredients

- ¼ cup (50 ml) unsweetened coconut cream
- ½ cup (75 gr) almond flour
- ½ cup (75 gr) mushroom, sliced
- ½ medium onion, chopped
- 1 tablespoon (1 bunch) of chives, chopped
- 2 tbsp. (30 ml) heart-healthy oil
- 4 large eggs, beaten
- Salt and pepper to taste

Directions:

8. Preheat the air fryer to 350°F/180°C for 5 minutes.
9. In a clean mixing bowl, combine the almond flour and heart-healthy oil.
10. Press the almond flour mixture at the bottom of a heatproof baking dish. Place in your air fryer and cook for 5 minutes.
11. Meanwhile, combine the rest of the ingredients in a mixing bowl.

Take the crust out and pour over the egg mixture.

12. Put the baking dish back into the air fryer and cook for 15 minutes at 350°F/180°C. Serve and enjoy!

Nutritional Fact Per Serving: Calories: 130; Carbohydrates: 3.5 g; Protein: 5.1 g; Fat: 11.1 g; Sugar: 1.1 g; Sodium: 37 mg; Fibre: 1.6 g

15.   Ham and Egg Crescents

Servings: 2

Prep Time: 15 minutes

Cooking Time: 10 minutes

Ingredients

- 2 tsp. butter
- 1 large egg
- 1 oz. (25 gr) chopped thinly sliced deli ham
- 2 tsp. 2% milk
- 2 tbsp. (25 gr) shredded cheddar cheese
- 1 tube (4 oz. –/100 gr) refrigerated crescent rolls dough

Directions:

1. Preheat the air fryer to about 300°F/150°C.
2. Combine the egg and milk in a small bowl.
3. Heat the butter in a small skillet until it is hot.

4. Cook, stirring the egg mixture over medium heat until the eggs are fully set. Turn off the heat.
5. Combine the cheese and ham in a mixing bowl.
6. Make two rectangles out of crescent dough. Perforations should be sealed, and half of the filling should be spooned down the centre of each rectangle.
7. Fold the dough over the filling and pinch the edges to seal.
8. Place in an air-fryer basket in a single layer on the greased tray.
9. Cook for 8–10 minutes, or until golden brown.

Nutritional Fact Per Serving: Calories: 326; Carbs: 3.5 g

16. Heart-warming Breakfast Buns

Servings: 4

Prep Time: 30 min

Cooking time: 25 min

Ingredients:

- 2 tsp. Baking powder
- 1 tsp. Cinnamon
- Egg white/whole egg, beaten (1 piece)
- 1 cup (150 gr) Flour, all-purpose, unbleached, whole wheat/gluten-free
- 1 cup (250 gr) Greek yogurt, non-fat, plain
- 1/2 teaspoon Kosher salt
- 3 tbsp. (40 gr) Raisins
- 2 tbsp. (25 gr) Raw sugar

Icing (reserve half):

- Water/milk (1 teaspoon)
- 1/4 cup (120 gr) Powdered sugar

Directions:

1. Prepare the icing by whisking together the milk and powdered sugar. Pour the smooth mixture into a Ziploc bag.
2. Set the air fryer at 325°F/160°C to preheat.
3. Cook the iced rolls in the air fryer for eleven to twelve minutes. Let cool.
4. Trim off the tip of the icing bag. Pipe the icing onto the rolls' surfaces in your desired pattern.

Nutritional Fact Per Serving: Calories 230 Fat 0.5 g Protein 10.5 g Carbohydrates 46.0 g

17. Mushroom Breakfast Casserole

Servings: 4

Prep Time: 5 minutes

Cooking Time: 20 minutes

Ingredients

- ½ cup (80 gr) mushroom, chopped
- 1 cup (250 gr) coconut cream
- 1 tsp. onion powder
- 2 tbsp. (25 gr) butter
- 8 large eggs, beaten
- Cooking spray
- Salt and pepper to taste

Directions:

1. Preheat the air fryer to 310°F/150 °C for 5 minutes.
2. Mix the eggs, butter, and coconut cream in a mixing bowl.
3. Pour in a greased baking dish together with the mushrooms and onion powder.
4. Season with salt and pepper to taste.
5. Place in the air fryer chamber and cook for 20 minutes at 310°F/150 °C.
6. Serve and enjoy!

Nutritional Fact Per Serving: Calories: 318; Carbohydrates: 3.8 g; Protein: 13.4 g; Fat: 27.8 g; Sugar: 1.6 g; Sodium: 203 mg; Fibre: 0.5 g

18. Scrambled Eggs

Servings: 2

Prep Time: 5 minutes

Cooking Time: 10 minutes

Ingredients

- 2 large eggs, beaten
- 2 tbsp. (25 gr) unsalted butter, melted
- Cooking spray
- Salt and pepper to taste

Directions:

1. Preheat the air fryer to 250°F/120°C for 5 minutes.
2. Mix all ingredients in a mixing bowl until well combined.
3. Place in a greased pan that will fit in the air fryer.
4. Cook for 10 minutes at 250°F/120°C.
5. Open the air fryer every 2 minutes and fluff with a fork.
6. Once done, serve warm and enjoy!

Nutritional Fact Per Serving: Calories: 174; Carbohydrates: 0.4 g; Protein: 6.5 g; Fat: 16.5 g; Sugar: 0.2 g; Sodium: 73 mg; Fibre: 0 g

19. Savory Cheese and Bacon Muffins

Servings: 4

Prep Time: 5 minutes

Cooking Time: 17 minutes

Ingredients:

- ½ cup (120 ml) of milk
- ½ cup (100 gr) of shredded cheddar cheese
- ½ teaspoon of onion powder
- 1 ½ cup (225 gr) of all-purpose flour
- 1 teaspoon (1 bunch) of freshly chopped parsley
- 1 teaspoon black pepper
- 1 teaspoon salt
- 1 thinly chopped onion
- 2 eggs
- A pinch of baking powder
- 4 cooked and chopped bacon slices

Directions:

1. Turn on your air fryer to 360°F/180°C.
2. Add and stir all the ingredients using a large bowl until it mixes properly.
3. Then grease the muffin cups with a non-stick cooking spray or line them with a parchment paper. Pour the batter proportionally into each muffin cup.
4. Place it inside your air fryer and bake it for 15 minutes
5. After that, carefully remove it from your air fryer and allow it to chill. Serve and enjoy!

Nutritional Fact Per Serving: Calories 180 Fat 18g Carbs 16g Protein 15g

APPETIZERS & SNACKS

20. Air Fried Kale Chips

Servings: 2

Prep Time: 5 minutes

Cooking Time: 10 minutes

Ingredients

- 1 bunch of kale, chopped into large pieces
- 1 teaspoon garlic powder
- 2 tbsp. (25 gr) almond flour
- 2 tbsp. (30 ml) olive oil
- Salt and pepper to taste

Directions:

1. Preheat the air fryer to 350°F/180°C for 5 minutes.
2. In a bowl, combine all ingredients until the kale leaves are coated with the other ingredients.
3. Place in a fryer basket and cook for 10 minutes at 350°F/180°C until crispy.

4. Serve and enjoy!

Nutritional Fact Per Serving: Calories: 220; Carbohydrates: 13.5 g; Protein: 5.5 g; Fat: 18 g; Sugar: 2.8 g; Sodium: 46 mg; Fibre: 4.9 g

21. All-Crisp Sweet Potato Skins

Servings: 3

Prep Time: 10 min

Cooking time: 50 min

Ingredients:

- 1 cup (200 gr) Black beans, fat-free, re-fried
- A pinch of Black pepper, freshly ground
- 3/4 cup (100 gr) Cheese, cheddar, reduced-fat, shredded
- (1 tablespoon) Cilantro, chopped
- Cooking spray, olive oil
- 3/4 cup (200 ml) Salsa
- A pinch of Salt, kosher
- Scallions, sliced thinly (2 pieces)
- Sweet potatoes, small (6 pieces)
- 1/2 tablespoon (10 ml) Taco seasoning

Directions:

1. Set the air fryer at 370°F/190 °C to preheat.

2. Cover the sweet potatoes in parchment and cook in the air fryer for thirty minutes. Let cool.

3. Mix the taco seasoning and black beans.

4. Halve the cooled sweet potatoes and remove most of the flesh. Spray the skins with cooking spray, sprinkle with pepper and salt, and air-fry for two to three minutes.

5. Fill each skin with black beans, salsa, and cheese. Return to your air fryer and cook for two minutes.

6. Serve topped with cilantro and scallions.

Nutritional Fact Per Serving Calories 150.5 Fat 6.0 g Protein 8.0 g Carbohydrates 25.0 g

22. Bacon Bites

Servings: 4

Prep Time: 10 min

Cooking time: 13 min

Ingredients:

- 1 pound (450 gr) Chicken breast, sliced into one-inch chunks
- 1/2 tablespoon Chili powder
- Bacon slices, cut into 1/3-portions (6 pieces)
- 1/3 cup (100 gr) Brown sugar
- A pinch of Cayenne pepper

Directions:

1. Stick a bacon piece onto a chicken piece, then roll to secure, finishing by piercing with a toothpick.
2. Repeat with the remaining bacon and chicken pieces.
3. Mix the brown sugar, cayenne pepper, and chili powder, then season the chicken bacon bites.
4. Cook in the air fryer for fifteen minutes at 500°F/250 °C.

Nutritional Fact Per Serving: Calories 339 Fat 16.0 g Protein 28.0 g Carbohydrates 18.0 g

23. Baked Eggplant Chips

Servings: 4

Prep Time: 5 minutes

Cooking Time: 15 minutes

Ingredients:

- 1 tablespoon (15 gr) grated goat cheese
- Egg whites
- 1/2 cup (150 gr) crushed cornflakes
- medium eggplant, cut into 1/4-inch/ 0,5 cm slices
- A pinch of ground black pepper

Directions:

1. Preheat the air fryer toaster oven to 245°F/120°C. Mix the crushed cornflakes, pepper, and goat cheese in a small container. Set aside the egg whites in a different container.
2. Dip the eggplant slices in the egg white and cover the crushed cornflakes mixture.
3. Place on a greased baking sheet. Bake in the preheated air fryer toaster oven for 5 minutes, then turn and bake for another 5 to 10 minutes until golden yellow and crispy.

Nutritional Fact Per Serving: Calories: 92 kcal Fat: 2.1g Carbs: 13.9g Protein: 5.9g

24. Coconut Chicken Bites

Servings: 4

Prep Time: 10 minutes

Cooking Time: 15 minutes

Ingredients:

- ¾ cup (75 gr) coconut, shredded
- ¾ cup (120 gr) panko bread crumbs
- 2 eggs
- 2 tsp. garlic powder
- 8 chicken tenders
- Cooking spray
- Salt and black pepper to the taste

Directions:

1. Mix pepper, salt, and eggs with garlic powder using a bucket and whisk well.

2. In another bowl, mix coconut with panko and stir well.
3. Dip the chicken tenders in the egg mix and then coat in coconut one well.
4. Spray chicken bites with cooking spray, place them in your air fryer's basket, and cook them at 350°F/180 °C for 10 minutes.
5. Serve and enjoy!

Nutritional Fact Per Serving: Calories: 252 kcal Fat: 4g Carbs: 14g Protein: 24g

25. Cheese Sticks

Servings: 6

Prep Time: 10 min

Cooking time: 7 min

Ingredients:

- 6 snack-size cheese sticks
- ¼ cup (30 gr) grated Parmesan cheese
- 1 teaspoon Italian Seasoning
- 1 teaspoon garlic powder
- 2 large eggs
- ¼ cup (30 gr) whole-wheat flour
- 1/4 teaspoon / a pinch of ground rosemary

Directions:

1. Unwrap the sticks of cheese and set them aside.

2. With a fork, crack and beat the eggs in a small bowl that is broad enough to match the length of the cheese sticks.
3. Mix the flour, Parmesan cheese, and seasonings in another bowl (or plate).
4. Roll the cheese sticks into the egg and then into the flour mix. Repeat until it is well covered all around the cheese sticks.
5. Place them in your air fryer's basket, ensuring they do not touch.
6. Cook as directed by your air fryer. The temperature should be 370°F/190°C and fry for 6–7 minutes. Serve with marinara sauce.

Nutritional Fact Per Serving: Calories 67 Fat 11.0 g Protein 3.0 g Carbs 12.0 g

26. Chocolatey Churros

Servings: 12

Prep Time: 30 min

Cooking time: 55 min

Ingredients:

- Baking chocolate, bittersweet, chopped finely (4 ounces / 100 gr)
- Vanilla Kefir (2 tbsp. /30 ml)
- Eggs, large (2 pieces)
- Cinnamon, ground (2 tsp.)
- Heavy cream (3 tbsp. / 50 ml)
- Water (1/2 cup / 120 ml)
- Flour, all purpose (1/2 cup / 75 gr)

- Sugar, granulated (1/3 cup / 75 gr)
- Salt, kosher (a pinch)
- Butter, unsalted, divided (1/4 cup + 2 tbsp. / 60 gr+ 25 gr)

Directions:

1. Combine the butter (1/4 cup / 60 gr) with salt and water. Let the mixture boil before stirring in the flour. Cook on a simmer until a smooth dough forms. Cook for another three minutes.
2. Place cooked dough in a bowl. Give it a constant stir until a bit cool, then add one egg at a time as you keep stirring.
3. Place the smooth batter in a piping bag and chill for half an hour.
4. Pipe 3-inch / 8 cm-long churro-shaped pieces of the batter into the air fryer basket. Cook for ten minutes at 380°F/190°C.
5. Mix the cinnamon and sugar. Brush the remaining butter (2 tbsp. / 25 gr) over the cooked churros before rolling in the cinnamon sugar.
6. Melt the cream and chocolate in the microwave, then stir in the kefir. Serve churros drizzled with the chocolate sauce.

Nutritional Fact Per Serving: Calories 173 Fat 11.0 g Protein 3.0 g Carbohydrates 12.0 g

27. Cinnamon Banana Bread

Servings: 8

Prep Time: 15 minutes

Cooking Time: 20 minutes

Ingredients:

- 1 teaspoon baking soda
- 1 teaspoon baking powder
- 1 teaspoon ground cinnamon
- 1 teaspoon salt
- ½ cup / 120 ml milk
- ½ cup / 120 ml olive oil
- 3 bananas, peeled and sliced
- 1 1/3 cups / 200 gr flour
- 2/3 cup / 150 gr sugar

Directions:

1. Add all the ingredients and mix well in the stand mixer bowl.
2. Grease a loaf pan. Place the mixture into the prepared pan. Press the Air Fry "Power Button" and turn the dial to select the "Air Crisp" mode.
3. Once you've set the cooking time at 20 minutes, press the Time button again and spin the dial to set the temperature to 330°F/160°C. Then press the Temp button and revolve the dial. To begin, click "Start/Pause."
4. Open the lid when the unit beeps to show that it is preheated. Arrange the pan in the "Air Fry Basket" and insert it into the oven.

5. After removing the pan from the oven, allow 10 minutes of cooling on a wire rack. Before slicing, carefully transfer the bread onto a wire rack to cool.
6. Cut the bread into desired-sized slices and serve.

Nutritional Fact Per Serving: Calories 295 Fat 13.3g Carbs 44 g Protein 3.1 g

28. Feta Fries Overload

Servings: 2

Prep Time: 5 min

Cooking time: 30 min

Ingredients:

- Potatoes, russet/Yukon gold, 7-ounce / 200 gr, scrubbed, dried (2 pieces)
- Lemon zest, freshly grated (2 tsp.)
- Chicken breast, rotisserie, skinless, shredded (2 ounces / 50 gr)
- Cooking spray
- Olive oil, extra virgin (1 tablespoon / 15 ml)
- Feta cheese, grated finely (2 ounces / 50 gr)
- Red onion, chopped (2 tbsp. / 50 gr)
- Parsley, flat-leaf, fresh, chopped (1/2 tablespoon / 1 bunch)
- Oregano, fresh, chopped (1/2 tablespoon / 1 bunch)
- Oregano, dried (1/2 tablespoon)

- Salt, kosher (1/4 tablespoon)
- Black pepper, freshly ground (1/4 tablespoon)
- Plum tomatoes, seeded, diced (1/4 cup / 8-10)
- Onion powder (1 pinch)
- Garlic powder (1 pinch)
- Paprika (1 pinch)
- Tzatziki, prepared (1/4 cup / 50 gr)

Directions:

1. Set the air fryer at 380°F/190°C to preheat.
2. Slice the potatoes into quarter-inch / 0,5 cm-thick fries. Add to a bowl filled with salt, pepper, onion powder, dried oregano, garlic powder, paprika, and zest, then toss until well-coated.
3. Cook potato fries in the air fryer for fifteen minutes.
4. Serve topped with feta cheese, shredded chicken, tzatziki, diced plum tomatoes, chopped red onion, and fresh herbs.

Nutritional Fact Per Serving: Calories 383 Fat 16.0 g Protein 19.0 g Carbohydrates 42.0 g

29. Old Bay Chicken Wings

Servings: 4

Prep Time: 5 minutes

Cooking Time: 25 minutes

Ingredients

- ½ cup / 100 gr butter
- ¾ cup / 120 gr almond flour
- 1 tablespoon/ 10 gr old bay spices
- 1 teaspoon lemon juice, freshly squeezed
- 16 pieces of chicken wings
- Salt and pepper to taste

Directions:

1. Preheat the air fryer at 350°F/180°C for 5 minutes.
2. Add all listed ingredients to a bowl, except butter, and stir well.
3. Place in the air fryer basket and cook for 25 minutes at 350°F/180°C.
4. Halfway through the cooking time, shake the fryer basket for even cooking.
5. Once cooked, drizzle with melted butter. Serve and enjoy!

Nutritional Fact Per Serving: Calories: 647; Carbohydrates: 5 g; Protein: 28.8 g; Fat: 58.8 g; Sugar: 1 g; Sodium: 1564 mg; Fibre: 2.8 g

30. Pesto Stuffed Mushrooms

Servings: 4

Prep Time: 10 minutes

Cooking Time: 15 minutes

Ingredients

- ¼ cup / 60 ml olive oil
- ½ cup / 60 gr cream cheese
- ½ cup / 60 gr pine nuts
- 1 cup / 20 basil leaves
- 1 tablespoon / 15 ml lemon juice, freshly squeezed
- 1-pound / 450 gr cremini mushrooms stalk removed
- Salt to taste

Directions:

1. Preheat the air fryer to 350°F/180°C for 5 minutes.
2. Place all ingredients except the mushrooms in a food processor and pulse until fine.
3. Scoop the mixture and place it on the side where the stalks were removed.
4. Place the mushrooms in the fryer basket.
5. Close and cook for 15 minutes at350°F/ 180°C. Serve and enjoy!

Nutritional Fact Per Serving: Calories: 289; Carbohydrates: 7.2 g; Protein: 5.8 g; Fat: 28.2 g; Sugar: 3 g; Sodium: 80 mg; Fibre: 1.2 g

31. Pita Bread Cheese Pizza

Servings: 4

Prep Time: 5 minutes

Cooking Time: 6 minutes

Ingredients

- 1 pita bread
- 1 tablespoon / 1/4 yellow/brown onion sliced thin
- 1 tablespoon / 15 ml pizza sauce
- 7 slices of pepperoni
- ½ teaspoon / 0,5 minced fresh garlic
- 1 drizzle of extra virgin olive oil
- ¼ cup / 100 gr mozzarella cheese
- 1 stainless steel short-legged trivet
- ¼ cup / 150 gr sausage

Directions:

1. Use the spoon and swirl some pizza sauce on the pita bread.
2. Insert your favorite cheese and toppings.
3. On top of the pizza, add a little more drizzle of some extra-virgin olive oil.
4. Place a trivet over Pita Bread in the Air Fryer. Cook for 6 minutes at 350°F/180°C
5. Finally, remove from the Air Fryer cautiously and cut.

Nutritional Fact Per Serving: Calories: 215; Carbs: 7.2 g; Protein: 5.8 g; Fat: 28.2 g

32.   Riced Cauliflower Balls

Servings: 2

Prep Time: 21 min

Cooking time: 9 min

Ingredients:

- Breadcrumbs (1/4 cup / 30 gr)
- Cauliflower rice, frozen (2 ¼ cup / 250 gr)
- Cheese, mozzarella, part-skim, shredded (1/2 cup / 75 gr)
- Cheese, parmesan/Pecorino Romano, grated (1 tablespoon)
- Chicken sausage, Italian, w/ casing removed (1 link / 100 gr)
- Cooking spray
- Egg, large, beaten (1 piece)
- Marinara, homemade (2 tbsp. / 30 ml)
- Salt, kosher (a pinch)

Directions:

1. Cook the sausage on medium-high until cooked through and broken up.
2. Stir in the marinara, salt, and cauliflower and cook for another six minutes over medium heat. Turn off the heat before stirring in the mozzarella.
3. Spray the cooled cauliflower mixture with cooking spray before molding it into 6 balls. Dip each ball in the beaten egg before coating it with breadcrumbs.
4. Load in the air fryer, coat with cooking spray, and cook for four to five minutes at 400°F/200°C on each side.

Nutritional Fact Per Serving: Calories 257 Fat 11.5 g Protein 21.5 g Carbohydrates 15.6 g

33. Savoury Chicken Nuggets with Parmesan Cheese

Servings: 4

Prep Time: 5 minutes

Cooking Time: 20 minutes

Ingredients:

- A pinch of kosher salt
- A pinch of seasoned salt
- A pinch of ground black pepper
- 1 lb. / 450 gr chicken breast, boneless, skinless, cubed
- 2 tbsp / 15 gr grated Parmesan cheese
- 2 tbsp / 30 ml olive oil
- 2 tbsp / 15 gr panko breadcrumbs
- 5 tbsp / 30 gr plain breadcrumbs

Directions:

1. Preheat the air fryer to 380°F/190°C and grease. Season the chicken with pepper, kosher, and seasoned salt; set aside. In a bowl, pour olive oil. In a separate bowl, add crumbs and Parmesan cheese.
2. Place the chicken pieces in the oil to coat, then dip into the breadcrumb mixture, and transfer to the air fryer. Work in batches if needed. Lightly spray chicken with cooking spray.
3. Cook the chicken for 10 minutes, flipping once halfway through. Cook until golden brown on the outside and no pinker on the inside.

Nutritional Fact Per Serving: Calories 312 Fat 8.9 g Carbs 7 g Protein 10 g

34. Shrimp and Chestnut Rolls

Servings: 4

Prep time: 10 minutes

Cooking time: 15 minutes

Ingredients:

- ½ pound / 250 gr already cooked shrimp, chopped
- 8 ounces / 200 gr water chestnuts, chopped
- ½ pounds / 220 gr shiitake mushrooms, chopped
- 2 cups / 200 gr cabbage, chopped
- 2 tbsp. / 30 ml olive oil
- 1 garlic clove, minced
- 1 teaspoon ginger, grated
- 3 scallions, chopped
- Salt and black pepper to the taste
- 1 tablespoon / 15 ml water
- 1 egg yolk
- 6 spring roll wrappers

Directions:

1. Heat a pan with the oil over medium-high heat, add cabbage, shrimp, chestnuts, mushrooms, garlic, ginger,

scallions, salt, and pepper, stir and cook for 2 minutes.

2. In a bowl, mix egg with water and stir well.

3. Arrange roll wrappers on a working surface, divide shrimp and veggie mix on them, seal edges with egg wash, place them all in your air fryer's basket, and cook at360°F/180°C for 15 minutes

4. Serve as an appetizer by transferring it to a serving tray... Enjoy!

Nutritional Fact Per Serving: calories 140, fat 3, fiber 1, carbs 12, protein 3

35. Sweet Popcorn

Servings: 4

Prep time: 5 minutes

Cooking time: 10 minutes

Ingredients:

- 2 and ½ tbsp. / 30 gr butter
- 2 ounces / 50 gr brown sugar
- 2 tbsp. / 30 gr corn kernels

Directions:

1. Put corn kernels in your air fryer's pan, and cook at 400°F/200°C for 6 minutes.

2. Transfer them to a tray, spread, and leave aside for now.

3. Heat a pan over low heat, add butter, melt it, add sugar and stir until it

dissolves. Add popcorn, toss to coat, take off the heat, and spread on the tray again.

4. Cool down, divide into bowls and serve as a snack.

5. Enjoy!

Nutritional Fact Per Serving: Calories 70, fat 0.2, fibre 0, carbs 1, protein 1

36. Walnuts Bowls

Servings: 4

Prep time: 10 minutes

Cooking time: 20 minutes

Ingredients:

- ½ teaspoon rosemary, dried
- ½ teaspoon sweet paprika
- 1 tablespoon / 15 ml olive oil
- 1 teaspoon chili powder
- 2 cups / 120 gr walnuts
- Salt and black pepper to the taste

Directions:

1. In a bowl, mix the walnuts with the rosemary, paprika, and the other ingredients, and toss to mix

2. Transfer it to your air fryer appliance and cook at 400°F/200°C for 20 minutes.

3. Divide into bowls; once done, serve and enjoy

Nutritional Fact Per Serving Calories 151, fat 1, fiber 6, carbs 10, protein 6

37. Zucchini Fries

Servings: 4

Prep Time: 5 minutes

Cooking Time: 15 minutes

Ingredients

- A pinch of garlic powder
- ½ cup / 75 gr almond flour
- 2 large egg whites, beaten
- 3 medium zucchinis, sliced into fry sticks
- Salt and pepper to taste

Directions:

1. Preheat the air fryer to 425°F/220°C for 5 minutes.
2. In a mixing bowl, combine the garlic powder and almond flour. Season with salt and pepper to taste.
3. Soak the zucchini in the beaten eggs and dredge in the almond flour mixture.
4. Place in the air fryer basket and cook for 15 minutes at 425°F/220°C.
5. Serve and enjoy!

Nutritional Fact Per Serving: Calories: 77; Carbohydrates: 5.2 g; Protein: 4.5 g; Fat: 5 g; Sugar: 2.3 g; Sodium: 22 mg; Fibre: 2.

POULTRY & TURKEY

38. Air Fried Lemon Chicken

Servings: 4

Prep Time: 5 minutes

Cooking Time: 30 minutes

Ingredients

- 1 tablespoon / 10 gr Spanish paprika
- 1 tablespoon / 10 gr stevia powder
- 2 tablespoon / 30 ml lemon juice, freshly squeezed
- 2 teaspoon / 1 minced garlic
- 3 tbsp. / 50 ml olive oil
- 4 boneless chicken breasts
- Salt and pepper to taste

Directions:

1. Preheat the air fryer to 325°F/160°C for 5 minutes.
2. Place all ingredients in a baking dish that will fit in the air fryer. Stir to combine.

3. Place the chicken pieces in the air fryer.
4. Cook for 30 minutes at 325°F/160°C.
5. Serve once it is done cooking, and enjoy!

Nutritional Fact Per Serving: Calories: 296; Carbohydrates: 1.9 g; Protein: 37.5 g; Fat: 14.8 g; Sugar: 0.3 g; Sodium: 92 mg; Fibre: 0.7 g

39. Casserole Turkey with Peas and Mushrooms

Servings 4

Prep Time: 10 minutes

Cooking Time: 20 minutes

Ingredients:

- 1 cup /70 gr of bread
- 1 cup /250 gr of mushroom soup
- 1 cup /250 gr of stock of chicken
- 1 stalk of celery hacked
- 1 yellow onion, sliced
- ½ cup / 70 gr of peas
- 2 lb / 1 Kg of turkey breasts, skinless and boneless
- Salt and black chili to taste

Directions:

1. Combine turkey with salt, pepper, onion, and celery in a saucepan that suits your Air Fryer. Place the peas and stock in the Air Fryer and cook at 360°F/180°C for fifteen minutes.

2. Add the mushroom soup and the bread cubes, stir, toss and prepare at 360°F/180°C for 5 minutes.
3. Divide between plates and serve sweet.
4. Enjoy!

Nutritional Fact Per Serving: Calories: 271, Fat: 9 g, Carbs: 16 g, Protein: 7 g.

40. Chicken Breasts and Tomatoes Sauce

Servings: 4

Prep time: 10 minutes

Cooking time: 20 minutes

Ingredients:

- ¼ cup /60 ml balsamic vinegar
- ¼ cup /30 gr parmesan, grated
- a pinch of garlic powder
- 1 red onion, chopped
- 14 ounces / 300 gr canned tomatoes, chopped
- 4 chicken breasts, skinless and boneless
- Cooking spray
- Salt and black pepper to the taste

Directions:

1. Spray a baking dish that fits your air fryer with cooking oil, add chicken, season with salt, pepper, balsamic vinegar, garlic powder, tomatoes, and cheese, and toss

2. Introduce in your air fryer and cook at 400°F/200°C for 20 minutes.
3. Divide among plates and serve hot. Enjoy!

Nutritional Fact Per Serving: calories 260, fat 14, fiber 11, carbs 19, protein 28

41. Delicious Chicken Parmesan

Servings: 4

Prep Time: 21 min

Cooking time: 9 min

Ingredients:

- Breadcrumbs, seasoned, whole wheat (6 tbsp. /40 gr)
- Butter, melted (1 tablespoon /15 ml) OR olive oil (1 tablespoon /15 ml)
- Chicken breast, halved, 200 gr (2 pieces)
- Cooking spray
- Marinara (1/2 cup /150 gr)
- Mozzarella cheese, reduced-fat (6 tbsp. /60 gr)
- Parmesan cheese, grated (2 tbsp. / 15 gr)

Directions:

1. Set your air fryer appliance to 360°F/180°C. Apply cooking sprays to the basket of the air fryer.
2. In a small bowl, combine breadcrumbs and parmesan cheese.

3. Fill another bowl with melted butter. Brush butter on chicken before dipping it in breadcrumb mixture.
4. Mist cooking sprays onto chicken before placing it in an air fryer. Cook for six minutes.
5. Top each piece with sauce, shredded mozzarella, and air-fry for another three minutes.

Nutritional Fact Per Serving: Calories 251 Fat 9.5 g Protein 31.5 g Carbohydrates 14.0 g

42. Fried Chicken Tenderloin

Servings: 4

Prep Time: 10 minutes

Cooking Time: 15 minutes

Ingredients

- ½ cup /75 gr almond flour
- 1 large egg, beaten
- 2 tbsp. /30 ml heart-healthy oil
- 8 chicken tenderloins
- Salt and pepper to taste

Directions:

1. Preheat the air fryer at 375°F/190°C for 5 minutes.
2. Season the chicken tenderloin with salt and pepper to taste. Soak in beaten eggs, and then dredge in the almond flour.

3. Place in the air fryer and brush with heart-healthy oil. Cook for 15 minutes at 375°F/190°C.
4. Halfway through the cooking time, give the fryer basket a shake to cook evenly.
5. Serve and enjoy!

Nutritional Fact Per Serving: Calories: 307; Carbohydrates: 3 g; Protein: 32.5 g; Fat: 18.3 g; Sugar: 0.7 g; Sodium: 85 g; Fibre: 1.8 g

43. Herbed Turkey Breast

Servings: 3

Prep Time: 15 minutes

Cooking Time: 35 minutes

Ingredients

- v dark brown sugar
- ½ teaspoon dried sage, crushed
- ½ teaspoon garlic powder
- ½ teaspoon paprika
- 1 bone-in, skin-on turkey breast (2½-pounds / 1 Kg)
- 1 tablespoon /15 ml olive oil
- 1 teaspoon dried rosemary, crushed
- 1 teaspoon dried thyme, crushed

Directions:

1. Mix the herbs, brown sugar, and spices in a bowl.
2. Coat the turkey breast evenly with oil and generously rub with the herb mixture.

3. Set the temperature of the Air Fryer to 360°F/180°C. Grease an Air Fryer basket.
4. Arrange turkey breast into the prepared Air Fryer basket, skin-side down.
5. Air Fry for about 35 minutes, flipping once halfway through.
6. Remove from Air Fryer and place the turkey breast onto a cutting board for about 10 minutes before slicing.
7. With a sharp knife, cut the turkey breast into desired slices and serve.

Nutritional Fact Per Serving: Calories: 688 Carbohydrate: 1.6g Protein: 81.2g Fat: 31.8g Sugar: 0.8g Sodium: 473mg

44. Smoked Chicken Mix

Servings: 4

Prep time: 5 minutes

Cooking time: 20 minutes

Ingredients:

- 1 tablespoon /1 bunch of cilantro, chopped
- 1 teaspoon chili powder
- 2 pounds / 1 Kg of chicken breasts, skinless, boneless, and sliced
- 2 tbsp. / 30 ml olive oil
- 2 tbsp. / 30 ml smoked paprika
- A pinch of salt and black pepper

Directions:

1. Mix the chicken with the paprika and the other ingredients in a bowl and toss.
2. Put the chicken breasts in your air fryer's basket and cook at 350°F/180°C for 10 minutes on each side.
3. Divide between plates, and serve with a side salad.

Nutritional Fact Per Serving: calories 222, fat 11, fiber 4, carbs 6, protein 12

45. Spicy Sweet Chicken Wings

Servings: 2

Prep Time: 10 min

Cooking time: 20 min

Ingredients:

- Chicken drumettes (10 pieces)
- Chili paste, freshly ground 1 teaspoon)
- Cooking spray
- Corn-starch (a pinch)
- Garlic, chopped finely (1 teaspoon)
- Ginger, fresh, chopped finely (1/2 teaspoon)
- Honey (2 tsp.)
- Kosher salt (a pinch)
- Lime juice, freshly squeezed ((1 teaspoon)
- Scallions, chopped (2 tbsp. / 0,5)
- Soy sauce, low sodium (1 tablespoon / 15 ml)

Directions:

1. Pat-dry, the chicken before coating it with cooking spray.
2. Cook in the air fryer for twenty-five minutes at 400°C/200 °C.
3. Whisk the corn starch and soy sauce together, then whisk in salt, sambal, lime juice, garlic, honey, and ginger. Heat to a simmer until thickened and bubbling.
4. Serve chicken coated with the sauce and sprinkled with scallions.

Nutritional Fact Per Serving: Calories 304 Fat 19.0 g Protein 23.0 g Carbohydrates 8.0 g

46. Spicy Chicken Taquitos

Servings: 12

Prep Time: 20 min

Cooking time: 10 min

Ingredients:

- 1 teaspoon cumin
- 1 teaspoon chili powder
- Kosher salt
- Cooking spray
- 3 cups / 450 gr shredded cooked chicken
- Freshly ground black pepper
- 1 chipotle in the adobo sauce, chopped
- 15 ml sauce

Rachel Vitale

- 1 block of softened cream cheese (8-oz. / 200 gr)
- 12 small corn tortillas
- 1 ½ cup / 150 gr shredded cheddar
- 1 ½ cup / 150 gr shredded Pepper Jack
- Pico de Gallo for serving
- 1 garlic clove
- Juice of lime
- Freshly ground black pepper
- Crumbled queso fresco for serving
- Salsa for serving

For the avocado cream

- 1 large avocado, pitted
- ½ cup / 120 gr sour cream
- 1/4 cup / 10 gr packed cilantro leaves
- Salt
- Pepper

Directions:

1. Combine the chicken, cream cheese, chipotle, sauce, cumin, and chili powder in a large bowl. With salt and pepper, season.
2. Place the tortillas on a secure microwave plate and cover them with a wet paper towel. Microwave for 30 seconds or before more pliable and wet.
3. Spread on one end of the tortilla about a quarter cup of filling, then scatter a little cheddar and pepper jack next to the filling. Repeat with the filling and cheese. Tightly roll-up.

4. Place in the air fryer basket, seam side down, and cook for 7 minutes at 400°F/200°C.
5. Serve with salsa, Pico de Gallo, and queso fresco with avocado cream.

For the avocado cream:

1. Mix the cilantro, avocado, sour cream, garlic, and lime juice into a food processor. With salt and pepper, season. Pour into a bowl, press directly over the top with plastic wrap, and refrigerate until ready to use.

Nutritional Fact Per Serving:

Calories 160 Fat 19.0 g Protein 23.0 g Carbs 8.0 g

47. Supreme Sesame Chicken

Servings: 4

Prep Time: 20 min

Cooking time: 15 min

Ingredients:

- Corn-starch, divided (1/3 cup + 2 tsp. / 40 gr + 10 gr)
- Soy sauce, reduced-sodium (2 tbsp. / 15 ml)
- Canola oil (1 ½ tablespoon / 20 ml)
- Chiles de árbol, seeded, chopped (3 pieces)
- White pepper, freshly ground (a pinch)

- Sesame seeds, toasted (1/2 teaspoon)
- Sugar (2 tsp.)
- Green onion, sliced thinly, divided (2 tbsp. / 1/4)
- Chicken thighs, skinless, boneless, patted dry, sliced into one-inch cubes (1 pound / 450 gr)
- Egg, large (1 piece)
- Salt, kosher (a pinch)
- Chicken broth, low-sodium (7 tbsp. / 100 ml)
- Ketchup (2 tbsp. / 30 ml)
- Rice vinegar, unseasoned 2 tsp.)
- Ginger, fresh, chopped finely (1 teaspoon)
- Garlic, chopped finely (1 tablespoon / 2)
- Sesame oil, toasted (1 teaspoon)

Directions:

1. Beat the egg before slathering it all over the chicken.
2. Mix the corn starch (1/3 cup / 40 gr) with pepper and salt. Add the egg-coated chicken and stir well
3. Place the chicken in the air fryer (preheated at 400°F/200°C) and cook for three to five minutes. Set aside to dry.
4. Whisk the remaining corn starch (2 tsp.) with sugar, broth, rice vinegar, ketchup, and soy sauce.
5. Cook the chiles in canola oil; once sizzling, stir in the garlic and ginger and cook for one minute.

Nutritional Fact Per Serving: Calories 302 Fat 13.0 g Protein 26.0 g Carbohydrates 18.0 g

48. Tasty Chicken Thighs

Servings: 4

Prep time: 10 minutes

Cooking time: 20 minutes

Ingredients:

- ¼ teaspoon of sugar
- ½ teaspoon white vinegar
- 1 tablespoon / 15 ml sherry wine
- 1 tablespoon /15 ml soy sauce
- 2 and ½ pounds / 1 kg of chicken thighs
- 2 tbsp. / 30 ml sesame oil
- 5 green onions, chopped
- Salt and black pepper to the taste

Directions:

1. Season chicken with salt and pepper, rub with half of the sesame oil, add to your air fryer and cook at 360°F/180°C for 20 minutes.
2. Meanwhile, heat a pan with the rest of the oil over medium-high heat, add green onions, sherry wine, vinegar, soy sauce, and sugar, toss, cover, and cook for 10 minutes
3. Shred chicken using 2 forks, divide among plates, drizzle sauce, and serve.
4. Enjoy!

Nutritional Fact Per Serving: calories 321, fat 8, fiber 12, carbs 36, protein 24

49. Tasty Turkey Fajitas

Servings:4

Prep Time:10 minutes

Cooking Time: 20 minutes

Ingredients:

- 1 jalapeno pepper, chopped
- 1 onion, sliced
- 2 bell pepper, sliced into strips
- 2 lime juice
- 1 tsp garlic powder
- 1 tbsp / 15 gr chili powder
- 1 lb / 450 gr turkey breast, boneless, skinless, and cut into 1/2-inch slices
- 1 1/2 tbsp / 20 ml tbsp olive oil
- 1/2 tsp onion powder
- 2 tsp oregano
- 1/2 tsp paprika
- 1/4 cup / 15 gr fresh cilantro, chopped

Directions:

1. Mix onion powder, garlic powder, oregano, paprika, cumin, chili powder, and pepper in a small bowl.
2. Squeeze one lime juice over the turkey breast, then sprinkle the spice mixture over the turkey breast. Brush turkey breast with 1 tbsp olive oil and set aside.
3. Add onion and bell peppers into the medium bowl and toss with the remaining oil.
4. Preheat the air fryer to 375°F/190°C.
5. Add onion and bell peppers into the air fryer basket and cook for 8

minutes. Shake basket and cook for 5 minutes more.
6. Add jalapenos and cook for 5 minutes. Shake basket and add sliced turkey over vegetables and cook for 8 minutes.

Nutritional Fact Per Serving: Calories 211 Fat 7.8 g Carbohydrates 16.2 g Sugar 9.1 g Protein 20.9 g Cholesterol 49 mg

50. Turkey Burrito

Serving 2

Prep Time: 12 min

Cooking time: 8 min

Ingredients:

- ½ red bell pepper, sliced
- 1 small avocado, peeled, pitted, and sliced
- 1/8 cup / 15 gr mozzarella cheese
- 2 eggs
- 2 tbsp. / 1 bunch of parsley
- 4 slices of turkey breast already cooked
- Salt and black pepper to the taste
- Tortillas for serving

Directions:

1. Whisk eggs to taste in a salt and pepper bowl, pour them into a saucepan, and put them in your Air Fryer basket. Cook at 400°F/200°C for 5 minutes, remove the saucepan from the fryer and switch eggs to a tray.

2. Arrange tortillas on a working board, spread eggs over them, and spread turkey meat, bell pepper, cheese, salsa, and avocado.

3. Roll out your burritos and put them in your Air Fryer after lining them with some tin foil.

4. Steam the burritos up at 300°F/150°C for 3 minutes, break them into plates and serve.

5. Enjoy!

Nutritional Fact Per Serving: Calories: 349, Fat: 23 g, Fibre: 11 g, Carbs: 20 g, Protein: 21 g.

51. Turkey Cakes

Servings 4

Prep time: 10 minutes

Cooking time: 10 minutes

Ingredients:

- 3lb. / 1 and 1⁄4 kg of turkey poultry, ground
- 1 teaspoon of crushed garlic
- 1 teaspoon of ground onion
- 6 champignons, split
- Cooking spray
- Salt and black chili to taste
- Tomato sauce

Directions:

1. Mix champignons with salt and pepper in your mixer and pulse well, then step into a bowl.

2. Whisk and add turkey, onion powder, garlic powder, salt, and pepper made from this blend.

3. Sprinkle with a cooking mist, pass it to the Air Fryer and cook for 10 minutes at 320°F/160°C.

4. Serve them side by side with tomato sauce and a savory side salad.

5. Enjoy!

Nutritional Fact Per Serving: Calories: 202, Fat: 6g, Fibre: 3g, Carbohydrates: 17g, Protein: 10g.

52. Turkey Legs

Servings: 2

Prep Time: 15 minutes

Cooking Time: 30 minutes

Ingredients

- 1 tablespoon /15 ml fresh lime juice
- 1 tablespoon / 1 bunch of fresh rosemary, minced
- 1 teaspoon fresh lime zest, finely grated
- 2 garlic cloves, minced
- 2 tbsp. / 30 ml olive oil
- 2 turkey legs
- Salt and ground black pepper, as required

Directions:

1. Mix the garlic, rosemary, lime zest, oil, lime juice, salt, and black pepper in a large bowl.

2. Add the turkey legs and generously coat with marinade. Refrigerate to marinate for about 6-8 hours.
3. Set the temp of the Air Fryer to 350°F/180°C. Grease an Air Fryer basket.
4. Place turkey legs into the prepared Air Fryer basket and Air Fry for about 30 minutes, flipping once halfway through.
5. Remove from Air Fryer and place the turkey legs onto the serving plates. Serve hot.

Nutritional Fact Per Serving: Calories: 458 Carbohydrate: 2.3g Protein: 44.6g Fat: 29.5g Sugar: 0.1g Sodium: 247mg

53. Turkey Meatloaf

Servings: 4

Prep Time: 20 minutes

Cooking Time: 20 minutes

Ingredients

- ¼ cup / 50 gr salsa Verde
- ½ cup / 30 gr fresh breadcrumbs
- ½ teaspoon dried oregano, crushed
- ½ teaspoon ground cumin
- 4 ounces / 100 gr of chopped green chilies
- 1 cup / 70 gr kale leaves, trimmed and finely chopped
- 1 cup / 120 gr Monterey Jack cheese, grated
- 1 cup/ 50 gr onion, chopped

- 1 egg, beaten
- 1 pound / 450 gr ground turkey
- 1 teaspoon red chili powder
- 2 garlic cloves, minced
- 3 tbsp. / 1 bunch of chopped fresh cilantro
- Salt and ground black pepper, as required

Directions:

1. In a deep bowl, put all the ingredients and mix until well combined with your hands.
2. Divide the turkey mixture into 4 equal-sized portions and shape each into a mini loaf.
3. Set the temp of your air fryer to 400°F/200°C. Grease an air fryer basket.
4. Arrange loaves into the prepared air fryer basket.
5. Air fry for about 20 minutes.
6. Remove from the air fryer and place the loaves onto plates for about 5 minutes before serving. Serve warm.

Nutritional Fact Per Serving: Calories: 435 Carbohydrate: 18.1g Protein: 42.2g Fat: 23.1g Sugar: 3.6g Sodium: 641mg

54. Turkey Wings

Servings: 4

Prep Time: 10 minutes

Cooking Time: 26 minutes

Ingredients

- 2 pounds / 1 kg of turkey wings
- 3 tbsp. / 50 ml olive oil
- 4 tbsp. / 50 gr chicken rub

Directions:

1. In a large bowl, mix the turkey wings, chicken rub, and oil using your hands.
2. Set the temperature of the Air Fryer to 380°F/190°C. Grease an Air Fryer basket.
3. Arrange turkey wings into the prepared Air Fryer basket.
4. Air Fry for about 25 minutes, flipping once halfway through.
5. Remove from Air Fryer and place the turkey wings onto the serving plates.
6. Serve hot.

Nutritional Fact Per Serving: Calories: 204 Carbohydrate: 3g Protein: 12g Fat: 15.5g Sugar: 0g Sodium:465mg

PORK, BEEF & LAMB

55. Baked Salsa Beef

Servings: 4

Prep Time: 15 min

Cooking time: 25 min

Ingredients:

- Salsa, chunky, thick (16 ounces / 400 gr)
- Cheddar cheese, shredded (1 cup / 120 gr)
- Ground beef, lean (1 pound / 450 gr)
- Biscuit mix (2 cups / 250 gr)
- Green onion, medium, chopped (1 piece)
- Milk (3/4 cup / 200 ml)

Directions:

1. Preheat the air fryer to 375°F/190°C.
2. Mist cooking sprays onto a square pan.
3. Cook beef until browned; drain before stirring in salsa, then spread in pan.
4. Stir together biscuit mix, cheese, onion, and milk to form a soft dough. Drop 12 tbsp. / 200 ml of dough on top of the beef mixture in the pan.
5. Air-fry for twenty-five minutes. Serve once done and enjoy.

Nutritional Fact Per Serving: Calories 212.5 Fat 11.5 g Protein 12.0 g Carbohydrates 15.5 g

56. BBQ Pork Ribs

Servings: 3

Prep Time: 5 hours

Cooking Time: 25 minutes

Ingredients:

- 1 lb. / 450 gr. pork ribs, cut into smaller pieces
- 1 tbsp Plus 1 tbsp / 15 ml + 15 ml maple syrup
- 3 tsp cayenne pepper
- 1 tsp oregano
- 1 tsp sesame oil
- 1 tsp soy sauce
- 2 cloves garlic, minced
- 3 tbsp / 50 ml barbecue sauce
- Salt and black pepper to taste

Directions:

1. Combine all the ingredients in a bowl, add the pork chops and leave to marinate for 5 hours
2. Preheat the Air Fryer Grill by selecting Grill/ air fry mode. Adjust temperature to 400°F/200°C and Time to 5 minutes
3. Remove the pork chops and arrange them on the grilling plate Transfer into the Air Fryer Grill

4. Air fry for 15 minutes, flip, and brush with the remaining 1 tbsp / 15 ml maple syrup. Air fry for additional 10 minutes
5. Serve and enjoy!

Nutritional Fact Per Serving: Calories: 346kcal, Fat: 11g, Carb: 5g, Proteins: 22g

57. Beef Fillet with Garlic Mayo

Servings: 4

Preparation Time:10 Minutes

Cooking Time: 40 Minutes

Ingredients:

- 1 cup / 230 gr mayonnaise
- 1/3 cup / 150 gr cup sour cream
- 1/4 cup / 20 gr chopped tarragon
- 2 cloves garlic (minced)
- 2 tbsp. / 1 bunch of chopped chives
- 3 lb. / 1,5 kg beef fillet
- 4 tbsp. / 65 gr Dijon mustard
- Salt and black pepper to taste

Directions:

1. Preheat the air fryer to 370°F/190°C.
2. Season beef using salt and pepper, transfer to the air fryer, and cook for 20 minutes. Remove and set aside.
3. In a bowl, whisk the mustard and tarragon. Add the beef and toss,

return to the air fryer and cook for 20 minutes.

4. Mix the garlic, sour cream, mayonnaise, chives, salt, and pepper in a separate bowl. Whisk and set aside.

5. Serve the beef with the garlic-mayo spread.

Nutritional Fact Per Serving: Calories: 400kcal, Fat: 12g, Carb: 26g, Proteins: 19g

58. Beef Pot Pie

Servings: 4

Prep Time: 10 minutes

Cooking Time: 30 minutes

Ingredients

- 1 cup / 120 gr almond flour
- 1 green bell pepper, julienned
- 1 medium onion, chopped
- 1 red bell pepper, julienned
- 1 tablespoon /15 gr butter
- 1 yellow bell pepper, julienned
- 1-pound / 450gr ground beef
- 2 cloves of garlic, minced
- 2 large eggs, beaten
- 4 tbsp. / ml heart-healthy oil
- Salt and pepper to taste

Directions:

1. Preheat the air fryer at 350°F/160°C for 5 minutes.

2. In a baking dish that will fit in the air fryer, combine the first 9 ingredients. Mix well, then set aside.

3. Mix the almond flour and eggs in a mixing bowl to create a dough.

4. Press the dough over the beef mixture. Place in your air fryer appliance and cook for 30 minutes at 350°F/160°C.

5. Serve and enjoy!

Nutritional Fact Per Serving: Calories per serving: 461; Carbohydrates: 9.8 g; Protein: 27.3g; Fat: 35.5 g; Sugar: 3.8 g; Sodium: 110 mg; Fibre: 3.3 g

59. Beef Tips with Onion

Servings: 2

Prep Time: 15 minutes

Cooking Time: 10 minutes

Ingredients

- ½ yellow onion, chopped
- 1 tablespoon / 15 ml avocado oil
- 1 teaspoon garlic powder
- 1 teaspoon onion powder
- 1-pound / 450 gr top round beef, cut into 1½- inch [4 cm] cubes
- 2 tbsp. / 30 ml Worcestershire sauce
- Salt and ground black pepper, as required

Directions:

1. Mix the beef tips, onion, Worcestershire sauce, oil, and spices in a bowl.
2. Set the temp of your Air Fryer to 360°F/180°C. Grease an Air Fryer basket.
3. Arrange the beef mixture into the prepared Air Fryer basket. Air Fry for about 8-10 minutes.
4. Remove from Air Fryer and transfer the steak mixture onto serving plates.
5. Serve hot.

Nutritional Fact Per Serving: Calories: 266 Carbohydrate: 4g Protein: 36.3g Fat: 10.5g Sugar: 2.5g Sodium: 192mg

60. Breaded Beef

Servings: 2

Prep Time: 10 minutes

Cooking Time: 10 minutes|

Ingredients:

- 1 egg
- 2 tbsp. / 30 ml Olive oil
- 4 beef
- 5 cups / 600 gr of breadcrumbs

Directions:

1. Preheat the Air Fryer Grill by selecting grill mode
2. Adjust temperature to 350°F/180°C and Time to 5 minutes

3. Whisk egg and olive oil ingredients in a bowl. Add breadcrumbs to another bowl and dip the beef in the egg mixture. Then coat with the breadcrumb mixture
4. Arrange on the grilling plate. Transfer into the Air Fryer Grill and grill for 12 minutes, flipping halfway
5. Serve with ketchup, and enjoy!

Nutritional Fact Per Serving: Calories: 256kcal, Fat: 5g, Carb: 12g, Proteins: 15g

61. Crispy Lamb

Servings: 4

Prep time: 10 minutes

Cooking time: 30 minutes

Ingredients:

- 1 egg,
- 1 garlic clove, minced
- 1 tablespoon / 10 gr bread crumbs
- 1 tablespoon / 15 ml olive oil
- 1 tablespoon / 1 bunch of rosemary, chopped
- 2 tbsp. / 15 gr macadamia nuts, toasted and crushed
- 28 ounces / 800 gr rack of lamb
- Salt and black pepper to the taste

Directions:

1. In a bowl, mix oil with garlic and stir well. Season lamb with salt and

pepper and brush with the oil. In another bowl, mix nuts with breadcrumbs and rosemary.

2. Put the egg in a separate bowl and whisk well.

3. Dip lamb in egg, then in macadamia mix, place them in your air fryer's basket, cook at 360°F/180°C and cook for 25 minutes, increase heat to 400°F/200°Cand cook for 5 minutes more.

4. Divide among plates and serve right away.

5. Enjoy!

Nutritional Fact Per Serving:

calories 230, fat 2, fiber 2, carbs 10, protein 12

62. Easy Pork Butt

Servings:4

Prep Time:10 minutes

Cooking Time: 20 minutes

Ingredients:

- 1 1/2 lbs. / 700 gr pork butt, chopped into pieces
- 1/4 cup / 120 gr jerk paste

Directions:

1. Spray the air fryer basket with cooking spray.

2. Add meat and jerk paste into the bowl and coat well. Place in refrigerator overnight.

3. Preheat the air fryer to 400°F/200°C.

4. Place marinated meat in the air fryer basket and cook for 20 minutes. Turn halfway through.

5. Serve and enjoy.

Nutritional Fact Per Serving:

Calories 339 Fat 12.1 g Carbohydrates 0.8 g Sugar 0.6 g Protein 53 g Cholesterol 156 mg

63. Garlic Lemon Pork Chops

Servings:5

Prep Time:10 minutes

Cooking Time: 20 minutes

Ingredients:

- 1 1/2 tbsp / 20 ml olive oil
- 1 tbsp / 1 bunch of fresh parsley
- 2 lbs / 1 Kg. pork chops
- 2 tbsp / 30 ml fresh lemon juice
- 2 tbsp / 2 garlic, minced
- Pepper
- Salt

Directions:

1. Mix garlic, parsley, olive oil, and lemon juice in a small bowl. Season pork chops with pepper and salt.

2. Pour garlic mixture over the pork chops, coat well, and allow to marinate for 30 minutes.

3. Add marinated pork chops into the air fryer basket and cook at 400°F/200°C for 20 minutes. Turn pork chops halfway through.
4. Serve and enjoy.

Nutritional Fact Per Serving:

Calories 623 Fat 49.4 g Carbohydrates 1.3 g Sugar 0.2 g Protein 41.1 g Cholesterol 156 mg

64. Glazed Pork Shoulder

Servings: 4

Prep Time: 15 minutes

Cooking Time: 18 minutes

Ingredients

- 1 tablespoon / 20 ml honey
- 1/3 cup / 200 gr soy sauce
- 2 pounds / 1 kg pork shoulder, cut into 1½-inch thick slices [4 cm]
- 2 tbsp. / 30 gr sugar

Directions:

1. Mix all the soy sauce, sugar, and honey in a bowl. Add the pork and generously coat with marinade. Cover and refrigerate to marinate for about 4-6 hours.
2. Set the air fryer temperature to 335°F/170°C. Grease an air fryer basket and place the pork shoulder into the prepared air fryer basket.
3. Air fry for about 10 minutes and then another 6-8 minutes at 390°F/200°C.

4. Remove from the air fryer and transfer the pork shoulder onto a platter.
5. Before serving, wrap the pork in a sheet of aluminum foil for approximately 10 minutes. Enjoy!

Nutritional Fact Per Serving:

Calories: 475 Carbohydrate: 8g Protein: 36.1g Fat: 32.4g Sugar: 7.1g Sodium: 165mg

65. Lamb and Eggplant Meatloaf

Servings: 4

Prep time: 5 minutes

Cooking time: 35 minutes

Ingredients:

- ½ teaspoon coriander, ground
- 1 egg
- 1 yellow onion, chopped
- 2 eggplants, chopped
- 2 pounds / 1 Kg lamb stew meat, ground
- 2 tbsp. / 1 bunch of cilantro, chopped
- 2 tbsp. / 30 ml tomato paste
- A pinch of salt and black pepper
- Cooking spray

Directions:

1. In a bowl, mix the lamb with the eggplants and the other ingredients except for the cooking spray and stir.

Rachel Vitale

2. Grease a loaf pan that fits the air fryer with the cooking spray, add the mix, and shape the meatloaf.
3. Put the pan in the air fryer and cook at 380°F/190°C for 35 minutes.
4. Slice and serve with a side salad.

Nutritional Fact Per Serving: calories 263, fat 12g, fiber 3g, carbs 6g, protein 15g

66. Lamb and Spinach Mix

Servings: 4

Prep time: 10 minutes

Cooking time: 35 minutes

Ingredients:

- ½ teaspoon of chili powder
- 1 pound / 450 gr lamb meat, cubed
- 1 pound / 450 gr spinach
- 1 red onion, chopped
- 1 teaspoon of garam masala
- 1 teaspoon of turmeric
- 14 ounces / 350 gr canned tomatoes, chopped
- 2 garlic cloves, minced
- 2 tbsp. / 12 gr ginger, grated
- 2 tsp. of cardamom, ground
- 2 tsp. of coriander, ground
- 2 teaspoon of s cumin powder

Directions:

1. Preheated air fryer and cook at 360 degrees F / 180°C.

2. In a heat-proof dish that fits your air fryer, mix lamb with spinach, tomatoes, ginger, garlic, onion, cardamom, cloves, cumin, garam masala, chili, turmeric, and coriander, and stir.
3. Introduce the mixture into the preheated air fryer and cook at 360 degrees F / 180°C for 35 minutes
4. Divide into bowls and serve. Enjoy!

Nutritional Fact Per Serving: calories 160, fat 6, fiber 3, carbs 17, protein 20

67. Lamb Racks and Fennel Mix

Servings: 4

Prep time: 10 minutes

Cooking time: 16 minutes

Ingredients:

- 1 tablespoon / 10 gr brown sugar
- 1/8 cup / 30 ml apple cider vinegar
- 12 ounces / 350 gr lamb racks
- 2 fennel bulbs, sliced
- 2 tbsp. / 30 ml olive oil
- 4 figs, cut into halves
- Salt and black pepper to the taste

Directions:

1. Mix fennel with figs, vinegar, sugar, and oil in a bowl, toss to coat well, and

transfer to a baking dish that fits your air fryer.

2. Introduce the mix to your air fryer and cook at 350 degrees F / 180°C for 6 minutes.
3. Season lamb with salt and pepper, add to the baking dish with the fennel mix, and air fry for 10 minutes more.
4. Divide everything into plates and serve.
5. Enjoy!

Nutritional Fact Per Serving: calories 240, fat 9, fiber 3, carbs 15, protein 12

68. Lamb Shanks and Carrots

Servings: 4

Prep time: 10 minutes

Cooking time: 45 minutes

Ingredients:

- 1 teaspoon of oregano, dried
- 1 tomato, roughly chopped
- 1 yellow onion, finely chopped
- 2 garlic cloves, minced
- 2 tbsp. / 30 ml olive oil
- 2 tbsp. / 30 ml tomato paste
- 2 tbsp. / 30 ml water
- 4 lamb shanks
- 4 ounces / 100 gr of red wine
- 6 carrots, roughly chopped
- Salt and black pepper to the taste

Directions:

1. Season lamb with salt and pepper, rub with oil, put in your air fryer, and cook at 360 degrees F / 180°C for 10 minutes.
2. In a pan that fits your air fryer, mix the onion with carrots, garlic, tomato paste, tomato, oregano, wine, and water, and toss.
3. Add lamb, toss, introduce it to your air fryer and cook at 370 degrees F / 190°C for 35 minutes.
4. Divide everything into plates and serve. Enjoy!

Nutritional Fact Per Serving: calories 432, fat 17, fiber 8, carbs 17, protein 43

69. Lamb with Tomatoes and Potatoes

Servings: 4

Prep time: 5 minutes

Cooking time: 25 minutes

Ingredients:

- 1 cup / 180 gr cherry tomatoes, halved
- 1 cup / 225 gr tomato sauce
- 1 tablespoon / 15 ml olive oil
- 1 teaspoon of rosemary, chopped
- 2 gold potatoes, peeled and cubed
- 2 pounds / 1 kg lamb stew meat, cubed
- A pinch of salt and black pepper

Directions:

1. Mix the lamb with the tomatoes and other ingredients in the air fryer's pan.
2. Put the pan in the machine and cook at 380 degrees F / 190°C for 25 minutes.
3. Divide between plates and serve.

Nutritional Fact Per Serving: calories 283, fat 12, fiber 3, carbs 6, protein 17

70. Low-Carb Casserole

Servings: 8

Prep time: 20 minutes

Cooking time: 25 minutes

Ingredients:

- 1 teaspoon of fennel seed
- 1 lb. / 450 gr ground sausage
- ¼ cup / 30 gr diced white onion
- ½ / 60 gr cup shredded Colby jack cheese
- Cooking spray
- 1 diced green bell pepper
- 8 whole eggs, beaten
- ½ teaspoon of garlic salt

Directions:

1. Brown the sausage in a skillet into your air-fryer.
2. Add the onion and pepper and simmer until the vegetables are soft

and the sausage is cooked, along with the ground sausage.

3. Spray an 8.75 inches / 22 cm pan and the air fryer with the cooking spray.
4. Place the mixture of ground sausages on the bottom of the pan.
5. Cover with cheese uniformly.
6. Pour the beaten eggs uniformly over the sausage and cheese.
7. Over the eggs, add fennel seed and garlic salt uniformly.
8. Put the dish straight into the air fryer's basket and cook at 390°F / 200°C for 15 minutes.
9. Remove and serve wisely

Nutritional Fact Per Serving: calories 182, fat 12, fiber 3, carbs 6, protein 17

71. Mustard Marina Ted Beef

Servings: 4

Prep Time:10 Minutes

Cooking Time: 45 Minutes

Ingredients:

- 1 tbsp. / 15 gr horseradish
- 1 tbsp. / 15 gr mustard
- 1-3/4 / 850 ml beef stock
- 2 tbsp. / 30 gr butter
- 3 cloves garlic (minced)
- 3 lb. / 1,5kg beef roast
- 3/4 cup / 180 ml red wine
- 6 bacon strips

- Salt and pepper to taste

Directions:

1. Preheat the air fryer to 400-degree F / 200°C.
2. Add the butter, horseradish, mustard, garlic, salt, garlic, and mix in a bowl. Rub the beef with the mixture.
3. Arrange the bacon on a cutting board, add the meat, and wrap the beef with the bacon strips. Put it into the air fryer, then cook for 15 minutes. Remove the beef roast and transfer to a pan.
4. Add the stock and wine to the pan, lower the temperature to 360°F / 180°Cand cook for 30 minutes.
5. Carve the beef and serve.

Nutritional Fact Per Serving: Calories: 350kcal, Fat: 9g, Carb: 27g, Proteins: 29g

72. Pork Tenderloin

Servings: 4

Prep time: 15 minutes

Cooking time: 30 minutes

Ingredients:

- 1 ½ lb. / 700 gr pork tenderloin
- 1 tbsp. / 15 ml olive oil

¼ t. of each:

- Garlic powder
- Pepper
- Salt

Directions:

1. Begin by removing the tenderloin from the fridge for 20 minutes before cooking. If silver skin is on the outside, remove the skin using a sharp knife.
2. In a small mixing bowl, combine garlic powder, pepper, salt, and olive oil and stir well.
3. Rub olive oil mixture on the outside of the tenderloin Place tenderloin in fryer basket and cook at 350°F / 180°C for 10 minutes, then flip. Frying until internal temp reaches 145°F / 63°C or approximately 8 to 10 minutes.
4. Take out of the fryer, and before slicing, allow pork to rest for 5 minutes.
5. Enjoy!

Nutritional Fact Per Serving:

Calories: 217, Net Carbs: 0.3 g, Fat: 7.2 g, Protein: 35.7 g

73. Steak Fajitas

Servings 6

Prep Time: 15 minutes

Cooking Time: 10 minutes

Ingredients:

- 1 large onion, halved and sliced

- 1 jalapeño pepper, seeded and minced
- 3 tbsp. / 1 bunch of minced fresh cilantro
- 2 tsp. of ground cumin, divided
- ¾ teaspoon / a pinch of salt, divided
- 2 large tomatoes, seeded and chopped
- ½ cup / 30 gr diced red onion
- 6 warmed whole wheat tortillas (8 inches / 20 cm)
- ¼ cup / 60 ml lime juice
- A beef flank steak of about 1-1/2 lbs / 700 gr.
- Optional: Sliced lime wedges and avocado

Directions:

1. In a small bowl, combine the first 5 ingredients; stir in 1 teaspoon / a pinch of cumin and 1/4 teaspoon / a pinch of salt. Allow it to stand until ready to serve.
2. Preheat the air fryer to 400°F / 200°C. Add remaining cumin as well as salt to the steak. In an air-fryer basket, place on a greased tray. Cook for 6–8 minutes per side or till meat attains desired doneness (a thermometer must read 135°F / 57°C for medium-rare, 140°F / 60°C for medium, and 145°F / 63°C for medium-well). Remove the basket from the oven and set it aside for 5 minutes.
3. In the meantime, place the onion on the tray in the air-fryer basket. Cook,

stirring once or twice, until crisp-tender, about 2–3 minutes. Thinly slice the steak across the grain and serve with onion and salsa in tortillas. Serve with avocado as well as lime wedges, if desired.

Nutritional Fact Per Serving:

Calories: 309, Fat: 7 g, Fibre: 2 g, Carbs: 13 g, Protein: 20 g.

74. Stuffed pork steaks

Servings 4

Prep Time:10 minutes

Cooking Time: 20 minutes

Ingredients:

- 1 cup / 20 gr of basil, minced
- 1 cup / 60 gr of chopped cilantro
- 1 orange juice
- 1 orange zest, grinded
- 1 tsp / 15 gr of dried oregano
- 2 chopped pickles
- 2 cumin spoons, ground
- 2 lemon juice
- 2 lime zest, rubbed
- 2 mustard spoons
- 4 garlic spoons
- 4 slices of ham
- 4 steaks from distant land pork
- 6 sliced Swiss cheese
- Olive oil: 3/4 cup / 180 ml
- Salt and black pepper to taste

Directions:

1. Blend lime zest and juice with orange peel in your mixing bowl, garlic, cilantro, oregano, mint, salt, cumin, and pepper, and blend well.
2. Coat the steaks with salt and pepper, put in a pan, attach the steaks marinade, and coat toss.
3. Put the steaks on a working surface, cut the pickles, cheese, mustard, and ham on them, with toothpicks, roll, and secure.
4. Place stuffed pork steaks in your frying pan and cook for 20 min at 340° F / 170°C.
5. Cut into plates and serve with a side salad.
6. Enjoy!

Nutritional Fact Per Serving:

Calories: 270, Fat: 7 g, Fibre: 2 g,
Carbohydrates: 13 g, Protein: 20 g.

FISH & SEAFOOD

75. 3-Ingredients Catfish

Servings: 4

Prep Time: 10 minutes

Cooking Time: 23 minutes

Ingredients

- ¼ cup / 40 gr seasoned fish fry
- 1 tablespoon / 15 ml olive oil
- 4 (6-ounces / 150 gr) catfish fillets

Directions:

1. Set the temp of your air fryer to 400 degrees F / 200°C. Grease an air fryer basket.

2. In a bowl, add the catfish fillets and seasoned fish fry. Toss to coat well. Then, drizzle each fillet evenly with oil.

3. Arrange catfish fillets into the prepared air fryer basket in a single layer. Air fry for about 10 minutes.

4. Flip the side and spray with the cooking spray. Air fry for another 10 minutes. Flip one last time and air fry for about 2-3 more minutes.

5. Remove from the air fryer and transfer the catfish fillets onto serving plates. Serve hot.

Nutritional Fact Per Serving: Calories: 294 Carbohydrate: 2.6g Protein: 28.7g Fat: 18.3g Sugar: 0g Sodium: 170g

76.   Air Fried Hot Prawns

Servings: 2

Prep Time: 5 minutes

Cooking Time: 5 minutes

Ingredients

- ½ teaspoon of ground black pepper
- ½ teaspoon of salt
- 1 teaspoon of chili flakes
- 1 teaspoon of chili powder
- 12 raw prawns, peeled and deveined
- 3 tbsp. / 50 ml olive oil

Directions:

1. Preheat the air fryer to 400-degree F / 200°C for 5 minutes.
2. Toss all ingredients in a bowl that will fit the air fryer.
3. Place the prawns in the air fryer basket and cook for 5 minutes at 400-degree F / 200°C.
4. Serve and enjoy!

Nutritional Fact Per Serving: Calories per serving: 222; Carbohydrates: 1.7 g; Protein: 7 g; Fat: 21 g; Sugar: 0.2 g; Sodium: 905 mg; Fibre: 0.7 g

77.   Air Fryer Calamari

Servings: 4

Prep Time: 15 minutes

Cooking Time: 15 minutes

Ingredients:

- 1 lb. / 450 gr calamari rings
- 2 cups / 150 gr panko breadcrumbs
- ½ cup / 75 gr flour
- 1 egg
- ¼ / 60ml cup milk
- 1 teaspoon of sea salt
- 1 teaspoon of pepper
- Non-stick cooking spray

Directions:

1. Preheat an air fryer to 400°F / 200 °C.
2. Place flour in the first bowl. Whisk egg and milk in a second bowl. Mix panko, salt, and pepper in a third bowl.
3. Coat calamari rings first in flour, then in egg, and finally in the panko.
4. Place half of the rings in the basket of the air fryer. Spray the tops with non-stick cooking spray.
5. Air fry for 4 minutes. Flip rings, spray with non-stick cooking spray, and cook for 3 minutes longer.
6. Repeat this for the other rings.

Nutritional Fact Per Serving: Calories: 310; Carbohydrates: 1.7 g; Protein: 7 g; Fat: 21 g; Sugar: 0.2 g; Sodium: 905 mg; Fibre: 0.7 g

78. Cajun Spiced Salmon

Servings: 2

Prep Time: 10 minutes

Cooking Time: 7 minutes

Ingredients

- ½ teaspoon of sugar
- 1 tablespoon / 15 ml Cajun seasoning
- 1 tablespoon / 15 ml fresh lemon juice
- 2 (7-ounces / 175 gr) (¾-inch / 2 cm thick) salmon fillets

Directions:

1. Set the temp of your air fryer to 356 degrees F / 180°C. Grease an air fryer grill pan.
2. Sprinkle the salmon evenly with Cajun seasoning and sugar.
3. Arrange fish into the prepared air fryer grill pan, skin-side up. Air fry for about 7 minutes.
4. Remove from the air fryer and place the salmon fillets onto the serving plates.
5. Serve immediately after drizzling with the fresh lemon juice.

Nutritional Fact Per Serving: Calories: 268 Carbohydrate: 1.2g Protein: 38.6g Fat: 12.3g Sugar: 1.2g Sodium: 164mg

79. Crab Cakes

Servings: 24 cakes

Prep Time: 15 minutes

Cooking Time: 10 minutes

Ingredients:

- 1 tablespoon / 15 gr sweet pickle relish
- 1 green onion, chopped
- 3 tbsp. / 50 gr reduced-fat mayonnaise
- a pinch of salt
- a pinch of prepared wasabi
- 1 finely chopped celery rib
- 2 large egg whites
- 1/3 cup + ½ cup / 30gr + 50gr dry breadcrumbs
- 1 ½ lump crabmeat, drained
- Cooking spray
- 1/3 cup / 80 gr reduced-fat mayonnaise
- ½ teaspoon of prepared wasabi
- 1 chopped celery rib
- 1 medium chopped sweet red pepper
- 3 finely chopped green onions
- a pinch of celery salt

Directions:

1. Preheat the air fryer to 375°F / 190°C. Combine the first seven ingredients in a mixing bowl; stir in one-third cup / 30 gr of breadcrumbs. Fold in the crab gently.

2. In a shallow bowl, place the remaining breadcrumbs. Into the crumbs, drop some heaping tbsp. of crab mixture. Coat the patties gently and form them into 3/4-inch-thick (2 cm) patties.
3. Put crab cakes in a single layer on a greased tray in the air-fryer basket in batches. Using cooking spray, spritz the crab cakes.
4. Cook for 8–12 minutes, until golden brown. Turning halfway through and spritzing with more cooking spray.
5. Meanwhile, combine the sauce ingredients in a food processor and pulse 2 or 3 times to blend or achieve consistency. Serve crab cakes with dipping sauce right away.

Nutritional Fact Per Serving: Calories: 49 Carbohydrate: 1.2g Protein: 38.6g Fat: 12.3g Sugar: 1.2g Sodium: 164mg

80. Creamy Tuna Cakes

Servings: 4

Prep Time: 15 minutes

Cooking Time: 15 minutes

Ingredients

- 2 (6-ounces / 150 gr) cans tuna, drained
- 1½ tbsp. / 20 gr mayonnaise
- 1½ tablespoon / 15 gr almond flour
- 1 tablespoon / 15 ml fresh lemon juice

- 1 teaspoon of dried dill
- 1 teaspoon of garlic powder
- ½ teaspoon of onion powder
- Pinch of salt and ground black pepper

Directions:

1. Mix the tuna, mayonnaise, flour, lemon juice, dill, and spices in a large bowl.
2. Make 4 equal-sized patties from the mixture.
3. Set the temperature of the air fryer to 400 degrees F / 200°C. Grease an air fryer basket.
4. Arrange tuna cakes into the prepared air fryer basket in a single layer. Air fry for about 10 minutes.
5. Flip the side and air fry for another 4-5 minutes.
6. Remove from the air fryer and transfer the tuna cakes onto serving plates. Serve warm.

Nutritional Fact Per Serving: Calories: 200 Carbohydrate: 2.9g Protein: 23.4g Fat: 10.1g Sugar: 0.8g Sodium: 122mg

81. Crispy Cod Sticks

Servings: 2

Prep Time: 20 minutes

Cooking Time: 7 minutes

Ingredients

- ¾ cup / 110 gr flour

- 1 green chili, finely chopped
- 2 garlic cloves, minced
- 2 tsp. / 4 ml light soy sauce
- 3 (4-ounces / 100 gr) skinless cod fillets, cut into rectangular pieces
- 4 eggs
- Salt and ground black pepper, as required

Directions:

1. In a shallow bowl, add the flour. Mix eggs, garlic, green chili, soy sauce, salt, and black pepper in another bowl.
2. Coat each piece with flour and then dip it into the egg mixture.
3. Set the temperature of the air fryer to 375 degrees F / 190°C. Grease an air fryer basket.
4. Arrange cod pieces into the prepared air fryer basket in a single layer. Air fry for about 7 minutes.
5. Remove from the air fryer and place the cod sticks onto serving plates. Serve warm.

Nutritional Fact Per Serving:

Calories: 483 Carbohydrate: 38g Protein: 55.3g Fat: 10.7g Sugar: 1.1g Sodium: 634mg

82. Fish and Chips

Servings: 6

Prep Time: 15 minutes

Cooking Time: 12 minutes

Ingredients

- 1 lb. / 450 gr Brussels sprouts halved
- 1 lb. / 450 gr potatoes
- 1 lb. / 450 gr cod fillets
- 2 tbsp. / 30 ml olive oil
- ½ teaspoon of pepper
- ½ teaspoon of salt
- 1/3 cup / 50 gr all-purpose flour
- 1 large egg
- 2 tbsp. / 30 ml water
- 1 cup / 75 gr crushed cornflakes
- 1 tablespoon / 10 gr grated Parmesan cheese

Directions:

1. Preheat the air fryer to 400°F / 200 °C.
2. Peel and cut potatoes into 1/2-in thick (1,5 cm) sticks.
3. In a bowl, toss potatoes with oil, pepper, and salt. Place potatoes in a single layer on a tray in the air-fryer basket.
4. Cook for 5 minutes until tender.
5. Toss potatoes and cook for 10 minutes until lightly browned and crisp.
6. In a second bowl, mix flour and half of the pepper. In a third bowl, whisk the egg with water. Toss corn flakes with cheese and the other pepper in a fourth bowl.
7. Sprinkle fish with salt and dip into flour mixture to coat both sides. Then dip in egg mixture and finally dip in cornflake mixture.

8. Remove fries from the basket and. Place fish in a single layer on a tray in the air-fryer basket and cook for 10 minutes until the fish is lightly browned, turning halfway through cooking.

9. Return fries to the basket to heat through. Serve immediately.

Nutritional Fact Per Serving: Calories: 330 Carbohydrate: 38g Protein: 55.3g Fat: 10.7g Sugar: 1.1g Sodium: 634mg

83. Lemon Garlic Shrimp

Servings: 2

Prep Time: 15 minutes

Cooking Time: 8 minutes

Ingredients

- a pinch of garlic powder
- a pinch of paprika
- ¾ pound / 350 gr medium shrimp, peeled and deveined
- 1 tablespoon / 15 ml olive oil
- 1 teaspoon of lemon pepper
- 1½ tbsp. / 20 ml fresh lemon juice

Directions:

1. Mix lemon juice, oil, and spices well in a large bowl. Add the shrimp and toss to combine.

2. Set the temp of your air fryer to 400 degrees F / 200°C. Grease an air fryer basket.

3. Arrange shrimp into the prepared air fryer basket in a single layer. Air fry for about 6-8 minutes.

4. Remove from the air fryer and transfer the shrimp onto serving plates.

5. Serve hot.

Nutritional Fact Per Serving: Calories: 260 Carbohydrate: 0.3g Protein: 135.6g Fat: 12.4g Sugar: 0.1g Sodium: 619mg

84. Pineapple Tuna Mix

Servings: 2

Prep time: 5 minutes

Cooking time: 20 minutes

Ingredients:

- 1 cup / 170gr cherry tomatoes, halved
- 1 cup / 170 gr pineapple, peeled and cubed
- 1 pound / 450 gr tuna fillets, boneless and roughly cubed
- 1 tablespoon/ 15 ml avocado oil
- 1 tablespoon / 15 ml balsamic vinegar
- 2 tbsp./ 30 gr capers, drained
- 2 tbsp. / 30 gr chives, chopped
- A pinch of salt and black pepper

Directions:

1. In a pan that fits the air fryer, mix the tuna with the pineapple, oil, tomatoes, and the other ingredients, and toss.
2. Put the pan in the fryer and cook at 390 degrees F / 200°C for 20 minutes.
3. Divide the mix into bowls and serve.

Nutritional Fact Per Serving: calories 280, fat 12, fiber 4, carbs 6, protein 11

85. Prawn Burgers

Servings: 2

Prep Time: 20 minutes

Cooking Time: 6 minutes

Ingredients

- a pinch of ground turmeric
- ½ cup / 60 gr breadcrumbs
- ½ cup /50 gr prawns, peeled, deveined, and finely chopped
- ½ teaspoon of garlic, minced
- ½ teaspoon of ginger, minced
- ½ teaspoon of ground cumin
- ½ teaspoon of red chili powder
- 2-3 tbsp. / 10 gr onion, finely chopped
- 3 cups / 200 gr fresh baby greens
- Salt and ground black pepper, as required

Directions:

1. Mix the prawns, breadcrumbs, onion, ginger, garlic, and spices in a large bowl.
2. Make small-sized patties from the mixture.
3. Set the temp of your air fryer to 390 degrees F / 200°C. Grease an air fryer basket.
4. Arrange patties into the prepared air fryer basket in a single layer. Air fry for about 5-6 minutes.
5. Remove from the air fryer and transfer the prawn burgers onto serving plates. Serve warm alongside the baby greens.

Nutritional Fact Per Serving: Calories: 240 Carbohydrate: 37.4g Protein: 18g Fat: 2.7g Sugar: 4g Sodium: 371mg

86. Pesto Haddock

Servings: 2

Prep Time: 15 minutes

Cooking Time: 8 minutes

Ingredients

- 1 tablespoon / 15 ml olive oil
- 1 tablespoon / 10 gr Parmesan cheese, grated
- 1/3 cup / 80 ml extra-virgin olive oil
- 2 (6-ounces / 150 gr) haddock fillets
- 2 tbsp. / 20 gr pine nuts
- 3 tbsp. / 5 gr fresh basil, chopped

- Salt and ground black pepper, as required

Directions:

1. Set the temperature of the air fryer to 355 degrees F / 180°C. Grease an air fryer basket.
2. Coat the fish fillets evenly with oil and sprinkle with salt and black pepper.
3. Arrange fish fillets into the prepared air fryer basket in a single layer. Air fry for about 8 minutes.
4. Meanwhile, for the pesto: add the remaining ingredients to a food processor and pulse until smooth.
5. Remove from the air fryer and transfer the flounder fillets onto serving plates. Top with the pesto and serve.

Nutritional Fact Per Serving: Calories: 606 Carbohydrate: 1.2g Protein: 43.5g Fat: 48.7g Sugar: 0.3g Sodium: 247g

87. Ranch Style Tilapia

Servings: 4

Prep Time: 15 minutes

Cooking Time: 13 minutes

Ingredients

- ¾ cup / 50 gr cornflakes, crushed
- 1 (1-ounce / 25 gr) packet dry ranch-style dressing mix*
- 2½ tbsp. / 40 ml vegetable oil
- 2 eggs

- 4 (6-ounces / 150 gr) tilapia fillets

Directions:

1. In a shallow bowl, beat the eggs.
2. Add the cornflakes, ranch dressing, and oil in another bowl until a crumbly mixture forms.
3. Dip the fish fillets into the egg and coat with the breadcrumb's mixture.
4. Set the temperature of the air fryer to 356 degrees F / 180°C. Grease an air fryer basket.
5. Arrange tilapia fillets into the prepared air fryer basket in a single layer. Air fry for about 12-13 minutes.
6. Remove from the air fryer and transfer the tilapia fillets onto serving plates. Serve hot.

Nutritional Fact Per Serving: Calories: 532 Carbohydrate: 4.9g Protein: 34.8g Fat: 41.8g Sugar: 0.7g Sodium: 160g

88. Salmon with Broccoli

Servings: 2

Prep Time: 15 minutes

Cooking Time: 12 minutes

Ingredients

- ¼ teaspoon / 4 gr corn-starch
- 1 (½-inch / 1,5 cm) piece fresh ginger, grated
- 1 scallion, thinly sliced
- 1 tablespoon / 15 ml soy sauce
- 1 teaspoon of light brown sugar

- 1 teaspoon of rice vinegar
- 1½ cups / 350 gr small broccoli florets
- 2 (6-ounces / 150 gr) skin-on salmon fillets
- 2 tbsp. / 30 ml vegetable oil, divided
- Salt and ground black pepper, as required

Directions:

1. Mix the broccoli, 1 tablespoon / 15 ml of oil, salt, and black pepper in a bowl.
2. Mix the ginger, soy sauce, vinegar, sugar, and corn starch well in another bowl.
3. Coat the salmon fillets evenly with the remaining oil and ginger mixture.
4. Set the temp of your air fryer to 375 degrees F / 190°C. Grease an air fryer basket. Arrange broccoli florets into the prepared air fryer basket.
5. Place the salmon fillets on top of broccoli, flesh-side down. Air fry for about 12 minutes.
6. Remove from the air fryer and place the salmon fillets onto serving plates. Serve hot alongside the broccoli.

Nutritional Fact Per Serving: Calories: 385 Carbohydrate: 7.8g Protein: 35.6g Fat: 24.4g Sugar: 3g Sodium: 628mg

89. Salmon with Shrimp & Pasta

Servings: 4

Prep Time: 20 minutes

Cooking Time: 18 minutes

Ingredients

- ½ pound / 150 gr cherry tomatoes, chopped
- 14 ounces / 350 gr pasta (of your choice)
- 2 tbsp. / 30 ml fresh lemon juice
- a bounch / 30 ml fresh thyme, chopped
- 2 tbsp. / 30 ml olive oil
- 4 (4-ounces / 100 gr) salmon steaks
- 4 tbsp. / 60 gr pesto, divided
- 8 large prawns, peeled and deveined

Directions:

1. Add the pasta to a large pan of salted boiling water and cook for about 8-10 minutes or until desired doneness.
2. Meanwhile, in the bottom of a baking dish, spread 1 tablespoon / 15 gr of pesto. Place salmon steaks and tomatoes over pesto in a single layer and drizzle evenly with the oil.
3. Now, add the prawns on top in a single layer. Drizzle with lemon juice and sprinkle with thyme.
4. Set the temp of your air fryer to 390 degrees F / 200°C. Arrange the

baking dish in the air fryer and air fry for about 8 minutes.

5. Once done, remove the salmon mixture from the air fryer. Drain the pasta and transfer it into a large bowl. Add the remaining pesto and toss to coat well.

6. Add the pasta evenly onto each serving plate and top with salmon mixture. Serve immediately.

Nutritional Fact Per Serving: Calories: 592 Carbohydrate: 58.7g Protein: 37.7g Fat: 23.2g Sugar: 2.7g Sodium: 203mg

90. Sesame Seeds Coated Haddock

Serving: 4

Prep Time: 15 minutes

Cooking Time: 14 minutes

Ingredients

- ½ cup / 60 gr breadcrumbs
- ½ cup / 25 gr sesame seeds, toasted
- a pinch of dried rosemary, crushed
- 2 eggs
- 3 tbsp. / 45ml olive oil
- 4 (6-ounces / 150 gr) frozen haddock fillets
- 4 tbsp. / 40gr plain flour
- Salt and ground black pepper, as required

Directions:

1. In a shallow bowl, place the flour. In a second bowl, add and whisk the eggs

2. In a third bowl, add the sesame seeds, breadcrumbs, rosemary, salt, black pepper, and oil until a crumbly mixture forms.

3. Coat each fillet with flour, dip into beaten egg, and coat with the breadcrumb's mixture.

4. Set the temperature of the air fryer to 390 degrees F / 200°C. Line an air fryer basket with a lightly greased piece of foil.

5. Arrange haddock fillets into the prepared air fryer basket in a single layer. Air fry for about 14 minutes, flipping once halfway through.

6. Remove from the air fryer and transfer the haddock fillets onto serving plates. Serve hot.

Nutritional Fact Per Serving: Calories: 497 Carbohydrate: 20.1g Protein: 49.8g Fat: 24g Sugar: 1.1g Sodium: 319g

91. Spicy Shrimp

Servings: 2

Prep Time: 13 minutes

Cooking Time: 5 minutes

Ingredients

- a pinch of cayenne pepper
- a pinch of smoked paprika

- a pinch of old bay seasoning
- ¾ pound / 350gr tiger shrimp, peeled and deveined
- 1½ tbsp. / 20 ml olive oil
- Salt, as required

Directions:

1. Set the temperature of the air fryer to 390 degrees F / 200°C. Grease an air fryer basket.
2. In a large bowl, mix well shrimp, oil, and spices.
3. Arrange shrimp into the prepared air fryer basket in a single layer. Air fry for about 5 minutes.
4. Remove from the air fryer and transfer the shrimp onto serving plates. Serve hot.

Nutrition Values (Per Serving)

Calories: 260 Carbohydrate: 0.3g Protein: 135.6g Fat: 12.4g Sugar: 0.1g Sodium: 619mg

92. Shrimp Tacos

Servings: 4

Prep Time: 15 minutes

Cooking Time: 15 minutes

Ingredients

- a pinch of salt
- 1 jalapeño pepper, seeded and minced, optional
- 2 large eggs
- 2 tbsp. / 30 ml 2% milk
- ½ cup / 75 gr all-purpose flour
- 1 ½ cup / 100 gr panko breadcrumbs
- 2 cups 400 gr coleslaw mix
- ¼ cup / 15 gr minced fresh cilantro
- 2 tbsp. / 30 ml lime juice
- 2 tbsp. / 40 gr honey
- 1 tablespoon / 5 gr ground cumin
- 8 corn tortillas (6 inches / 15 cm), warmed
- 1 tablespoon / 10gr garlic powder
- 1 lb. / 450 gr uncooked shrimp (41–50), peeled and deveined
- Cooking spray
- 1 medium ripe avocado, peeled and sliced

Directions:

1. Toss cilantro, coleslaw mix, lime juice, honey, salt, and, if desired, jalapeño in a small bowl to coat. Then set aside.
2. Preheat the air fryer to 375°F / 190°C.
3. Whisk the eggs and milk together in a shallow bowl. Then in a separate shallow bowl, place the flour. Combine panko, cumin, and garlic powder in a 3rd shallow bowl. Coat both sides of the shrimp in flour and shake off excess. Dip in the egg mixture, then in the panko mixture, patting to ensure that the coating sticks.
4. In a greased air-fryer basket, arrange shrimp in a single layer in batches; spritz with cooking spray. Cook for 2–3 minutes, or until golden brown. Spritz with cooking spray and turn.

Cook for another 2–3 minutes, till golden brown and shrimp, turn pink.

5. Serve the shrimp in tortillas along with coleslaw and avocado.

Nutrition Values (Per Serving) Calories: 456 Carbohydrate: 0.3g Protein: 135.6g Fat: 12.4g Sugar: 0.1g Sodium: 619mg

93. Sweet & Sour Glazed Salmon

Servings: 2

Prep Time: 20 minutes

Cooking Time: 12 minutes

Ingredients

- 3 tsp. / 15 ml rice wine vinegar
- 1 teaspoon / 5 ml water
- 4 (3½-ounces / 90 gr) salmon fillets
- 1/3 cup / 60 ml soy sauce
- 1/3 cup / 100 gr honey

Directions:

1. In a small clean bowl, mix the soy sauce, honey, vinegar, and water in another bowl, and reserve about half of the mixture.
2. Add salmon fillets to the remaining mixture and coat well. Cover the bowl and refrigerate to marinate for about 2 hours.

3. Set the temp of your air fryer to 355 degrees F / 180°C. Grease an air fryer basket.
4. Arrange salmon fillets into the prepared air fryer basket in a single layer.
5. Air fry for about 12 minutes, flipping once halfway through and coating with the reserved marinade every 3 minutes.
6. Remove from the air fryer and place the salmon fillets onto serving plates. Serve hot.

Nutritional Fact Per Serving: Calories: 462 Carbohydrate: 49.8g Protein: 41.3g Fat: 12.3g Sugar: 47.1g Sodium: 2000mg

VEGETARIAN MAIN

94. Balsamic Artichokes

Servings: 4

Prep Time:11 minutes

Cooking Time: 8 minutes

Ingredients:

- 2 tsp / 10 ml of balsamic vinegar
- Black pepper and salt
- 1/4 cup / 60 ml of olive oil
- 1 tsp of oregano
- 4 big trimmed artichokes
- 2 tbsp / 30 ml of lemon juice
- 2 cloves of garlic

Directions:

1. Sprinkle the artichokes with pepper and salt.
2. Brush oil over the artichokes and add lemon juice.
3. Place the artichokes on the Air Fryer Grill. Set the Air Fryer Grill at Air fryer/Grill, Timer at 7 minutes at 360-degree F / 180°C.
4. Mix garlic, lemon juice, pepper, vinegar, and oil in a bowl.
5. Add oregano and salt and mix well.
6. Serve the artichokes with balsamic vinaigrette.

Nutritional Fact Per Serving: Calories: 533kcal, Fat: 29g, Carb: 68g, Proteins: 19g

95.   Broccoli with Olives

Servings: 4

Prep Time: 15 minutes

Cooking Time: 19 minutes

Ingredients

- ¼ cup / 30 gr Parmesan cheese, grated
- 1/3 cup / 30 gr Kalamata olives, halved and pitted
- 2 pounds / 1 kg broccoli, stemmed and cut into 1-inch florets
- 2 tbsp. / 30 ml olive oil
- 2 tsp. / 30 ml fresh lemon zest, grated
- Salt and ground black pepper, as required

Directions:

1. Add the broccoli to a pan of boiling water and cook for about 3-4 minutes. Drain the broccoli well.
2. Set the temperature of the air fryer to 400 degrees F / 200 °C. Grease an air fryer basket.
3. Mix broccoli, oil, salt, and black pepper in a bowl.
4. Arrange broccoli into the prepared air fryer basket. Air fry for about 15 minutes, tossing once halfway through.

5. Remove from the air fryer and stir in the olives, lemon zest, and cheese. Serve immediately.

Nutritional Fact Per Serving: Calories: 169 Carbohydrate: 16g Protein: 8.5g Fat: 10.2g Sugar: 3.9g Sodium: 254mg

96.   Cheese Stuffed Tomatoes

Servings: 2

Prep Time: 15 minutes

Cooking Time: 15 minutes

Ingredients

- ½ cup / 80 gr broccoli, finely chopped
- ½ / 80 gr cup cheddar cheese, shredded
- ½ teaspoon of dried thyme, crushed
- 1 tablespoon / 15 gr unsalted butter, melted
- 2 large tomatoes

Directions:

1. Slice the top of each tomato and scoop out pulp and seeds.
2. In a bowl, mix the chopped broccoli and cheese. Stuff each tomato evenly with broccoli mixture.
3. Set the temperature of the air fryer to 355 degrees F / 180°C. Grease an air fryer basket.

4. Arrange tomatoes into the prepared air fryer basket. Drizzle evenly with butter and air fry for about 12-15 minutes.
5. Remove from the air fryer and transfer the tomatoes onto a serving platter.
6. Set aside to cool slightly. Garnish with thyme and serve.

Nutritional Fact Per Serving: Calories: 206 Carbohydrate: 9.1g Protein: 9.4g Fat: 15.6g Sugar: 5.3g Sodium: 233mg

97. Cheesy Brussel Sprouts

Servings: 3

Prep Time: 15 minutes

Cooking Time: 10 minutes

Ingredients

- ¼ cup / 30 gr Parmesan cheese, shredded
- ¼ cup / 30 gr whole wheat breadcrumbs
- 1 pound / 450 gr Brussels sprouts, trimmed and halved
- 1 tablespoon / 15 ml balsamic vinegar
- 1 tablespoon / 15 ml extra-virgin olive oil
- Salt and ground black pepper, as required

Directions:

1. Set the temp of your air fryer to 400 degrees F / 200 °C. Grease an air fryer basket.
2. Mix Brussel sprouts, vinegar, oil, salt, and black pepper in a bowl.
3. Arrange Brussel sprouts into the prepared air fryer basket in a single layer. Air fry for about 5 minutes.
4. Remove from the air fryer and flip the Brussel sprouts.
5. Sprinkle the Brussel sprouts evenly with breadcrumbs, followed by the cheese. Air fryer for about 5 more minutes.
6. Remove from the air fryer and transfer the Brussels sprouts onto serving plates. Serve hot.

Nutritional Fact Per Serving: Calories: 240 Carbohydrate: 19.4g Protein: 16.3g Fat: 12.6g Sugar: 3.4g Sodium: 548mg

98. Cherry Tomatoes Skewers

Servings: 4

Prep time: 30 minutes

Cooking time: 6 minutes

Ingredients:

- 1 tbsp. /3 gr thyme, chopped
- 2 tbsp. / 30 ml balsamic vinegar
- 2 tbsp. / 30 ml olive oil
- 24 cherry tomatoes
- 3 garlic cloves, minced

- 3 tablespoon + 2 tablespoon / 45 ml + 30 ml balsamic vinegar
- 2 tbsp. + 4 tbsp./ 20 ml + 40 ml olive oil

For the dressing:

- Salt and black pepper to the taste

Directions:

1. In a bowl, mix 2 tbsp. / 30 ml oil with 3 tbsp. vinegar / 45 ml, 3 garlic cloves, thyme, salt, and black pepper, and whisk well.
2. Add tomatoes, toss to coat and leave aside for 30 minutes. Arrange 6 tomatoes on one skewer and repeat with the rest of the tomatoes.
3. Introduce them to your air fryer and cook at 360 degrees F / 180°C for 6 minutes.
4. Mix 2 tbsp. vinegar / 30 ml with salt, pepper, and 4 tbsp. / 60 ml oil in another bowl and whisk well.
5. Arrange tomato skewers on plates and serve with the dressing drizzled on top. Enjoy

Nutritional Fact Per Serving calories 140, fat 1, fiber 1, carbs 2, protein 7

99. Chili Pepper Casserole

Servings: 2

Prep Time: 20 min

Cooking time: 30 min

Ingredients:

- Boiling water (1/3 cup / 80 ml)
- Bulgur, uncooked (2 tbsp. / 10 gr)
- Chile pepper, whole, roasted (8 ounces / 200 gr)
- Corn, whole kernel, frozen, thawed (1/3 cup / 60 gr)
- Garlic powder (a pinch)
- Jalapeno pepper, fresh, chopped (1/2 teaspoon)
- Marjoram leaves, dried (a pinch) OR marjoram, fresh, chopped (1 teaspoon)
- Mozzarella cheese, reduced fat, shredded (1/3 cup / 40 gr)
- Salsa, reduced sodium (1/4 cup / 40 ml)
- Yogurt, fat-free, plain (1/4 cup/ 40 ml)

Directions:

1. Preheat the air fryer to 325 degrees Fahrenheit / 160°C. Mist cooking sprays onto a baking dish.
2. Soak bulgur in water for ten minutes. Stir in cheese (1/4 cup / 30 gr), corn, garlic powder, jalapeno, and marjoram.
3. Slice chiles and remove seeds and ribs. Drain and stuff each with filling (1/4 cup / 40 gr).
4. Arrange stuffed chiles in a baking dish and top with the remaining cheese and salsa. Air-fry for twenty-five to thirty minutes. Serve each topped with a dollop of yogurt.

Nutritional Fact Per Serving: Calories 170 Fat 4.5 g Protein 9.0 g Carbohydrates 23.0 g

100. Fried Patty Pan Squash

Servings: 4

Prep time: 10 minutes

Cooking time: 15 minutes

Ingredients:

- ½ teaspoon of salt
- a pinch of dried oregano
- 1 tablespoon / 15 ml olive oil
- a pinch of dried thyme
- 5 cups / 125 gr halved small patty pan squash
- 2 minced garlic cloves
- a pinch of pepper
- 1 tablespoon / a bunch of minced fresh parsley

Directions:

1. Preheat the air fryer to 375°F / 190°C.
2. Squash should be placed in a large mixing bowl. Combine squash with salt, oil, garlic, oregano, thyme, and pepper. Toss to coat evenly.
3. In an air-fryer basket, place the squash on a greased tray. Cook, occasionally stirring, until the vegetables are tender, about 10–15 minutes.
4. Serve with parsley.

Nutritional Fact Per Serving: calories 58, fat 3, fiber 3, carbs 7, protein 3

101. Collard Greens Mix

Servings: 4

Prep time: 10 minutes

Cooking time: 10 minutes

Ingredients:

- 1 bunch collard greens, trimmed
- 1 tablespoon / 15 ml balsamic vinegar
- 1 teaspoon of sugar
- 1 yellow onion, chopped
- 2 tbsp. / 30 ml olive oil
- 2 tbsp. / 30 ml tomato puree
- 3 garlic cloves, minced
- Salt and black pepper to the taste

Directions:

1. Mix oil, garlic, vinegar, onion, tomato puree, and whisks in a dish that fits your air fryer.
2. Add collard greens, salt, pepper, and sugar to your air fryer and cook at 320 degrees F / 160°C for 10 minutes.
3. Divide collard greens, mix on plates and serve.
4. Enjoy!

Nutritional Fact Per Serving: calories 121, fat 3, fiber 3, carbs 7, protein 3

102. Mayo Buttered Carrot-Zucchini

Servings: 4

Prep Time: 10 minutes

Cooking Time: 25 minutes

Ingredients:

- 1 tablespoon / 3 gr grated onion
- 1/2 zucchinis, sliced
- 1/2-pound / 220 gr carrots, sliced
- 1/4 cup / 30 gr Italian bread crumbs
- 1/4 cup / 60 gr mayonnaise
- 1/4 cup /60 ml water
- a pinch of ground black pepper
- a pinch of prepared horseradish
- a pinch of salt
- 2 tbsp. / 30 gr butter, melted

Directions:

1. Place the instant pot air fryer lid on and lightly grease the baking pan of the instant pot with cooking spray.
2. Add carrots, place the baking pan in the instant pot, and close the air fryer lid.
3. Cook for 8 minutes at 360°F / 180°C. Continue cooking for another 5 minutes with the zucchini added in at this point.
4. Meanwhile, in a bowl, whisk well pepper, salt, horseradish, onion, mayonnaise, and water. Pour into the pan of veggies. Toss well to coat.
5. Sprinkle over veggies. Cook for 10 minutes at 390°F / 200°C until tops are lightly browned.

Nutritional Fact Per Serving: Calories: 223; Carbs: 13.8g; Protein: 2.7g; Fat: 17.4g

103. Potatoes (Unpeeled) And Yogurt Sauce

Servings: 4

Prep time: 10 – 20 minutes,

Cooking time: 30 – 45 minutes;

Ingredients:

- 1 onion
- 1 pepper
- 1 pinch of sweet paprika
- 1 1/2 tbsp / 20 g tomato sauce
- 3 ½ tbsp / 50 g lean yogurt
- 3 ½ tbsp 50 g of mayonnaise
- 1 ½ lbs / 750 g of fresh potatoes
- Basil at ease
- Salt taste

Direction:

1. Wash the potatoes and let them soak in cold water and baking soda for 15 minutes, and then brush them well with water.
2. Cut them in quarters and put them in the basket previously greased. Set the air fryer to 300°F / 150°C.

3. Cook the potatoes for 15 minutes, then add the chopped pepper and sliced onion; Salt.
4. Cook for 15 minutes, and then add the fresh basil cut to the menu. Cook for another 15 minutes.
5. If you want to accompany the potatoes with the yogurt sauce, simply mix all the ingredients until you get a creamy sauce.

Nutritional Fact Per Serving: Calories 49.1 Fat 2.5 g Carbohydrate 2.4 g Sugars 1.7 g Protein 4.1 g Cholesterol 5.2 mg

104. Rice spaghetti with vegetables

Servings: 4

Prep time: 10 – 20 minutes

Cooking time: 15 – 30 minutes

Ingredients:

- ½ cup / 100 g of bean sprouts
- 1 cup / 100 g of celery
- 1 1/3 cup / 150 g of carrots
- 2 cup / 150g kale
- 2 scallions
- 2 tbsp / 30 ml soy sauce
- 1 cup / 200 g of rice spaghetti

Direction:

1. Spray the basket of the air fryer. Cut all the vegetables in julienne and put the celery, chives, and carrots in the basket.
2. Set the air fryer to 300°F / 150°C. Cook for 10 minutes.
3. Add the sprouts and soy sauce and cook for another 10 minutes.
4. Meanwhile, cook the rice spaghetti in salted water and boil and serve with the previously prepared sauce.

Nutritional Fact Per Serving:

Calories 235.0 Fat 10.9 g Carbohydrate 34.7 g Sugars 6.4 g Protein13.9 g Cholesterol 0.5 mg

105. Spiced Eggplant

Servings: 3

Prep Time: 15 minutes

Cooking Time: 27 minutes

Ingredients

- 1 tablespoon / 15 ml fresh lemon juice
- 1 tablespoon/ 15 ml Maggi seasoning sauce
- 1 teaspoon of garlic powder
- 1 teaspoon of onion powder
- 1 teaspoon of sumac
- 2 medium eggplants, cubed
- 2 tbsp. / 30 gr butter, melted
- 2 tbsp. / 15 gr Parmesan cheese, shredded
- Salt and ground black pepper, as required

Directions:

1. Set the temperature of the air fryer to 320 degrees F / 160°C. Grease an air fryer basket.
2. Mix the eggplant cubes, butter, seasoning sauce, and spices in a bowl.
3. Arrange eggplant cubes into the prepared air fryer basket in a single layer. Air fry for about 15 minutes.
4. Remove from the air fryer and toss the eggplant cubes.
5. Now, set the temperature of the air fryer to 350 degrees F / 180°C and air fry for about 10-12 minutes, tossing once halfway through.
6. Remove from the air fryer and transfer the eggplant cubes into a bowl.
7. Add the lemon juice and Parmesan and toss to coat well. Serve immediately.

Nutritional Fact Per Serving: Calories: 173 Carbohydrate: 23g Protein: 4.6g Fat: 8.9g Sugar: 11.6g Sodium: 276mg

106. Spinach Pie

Servings 2

Prep Time 10 minutes

Cooking Time: 18 minutes

Ingredients:

- 1 tablespoon / 15 ml of olive oil
- 1 yellow onion, chopped
- 2 eggs
- 2 tbsp. / 30 gr of butter
- 2 tbsp. / 30 ml of milk
- 3 ounces / 75 gr of cottage cheese
- 7 ounces / 175 gr of flour
- 7 ounces/ 175 gr of spinach
- Salt and black pepper to the taste

Directions:

1. Mix the flour and butter, 1 egg, milk, salt, and pepper in your food processor, blend properly, move to a bowl, knead, cover, and leave for 10 minutes.
2. Heat a pan over medium heat with the oil, add the onion and spinach, stir and cook for 2 minutes.
3. Add salt, pepper, leftover egg, and cottage cheese, stir well and heat up.
4. Divide the dough into 4 bits, roll each slice, place it on the bottom of a ramekin, apply the spinach filling over the dough, put the ramekins in the basket of your Air Fryer, and cook for 15 minutes at 360° F / 180°C.
5. Serve warm. Enjoy!

Nutritional Fact Per Serving: Calories: 250, Fat: 12 g, Fibre: 2 g, Carbs: 23 g, Protein: 12 g.

107. Toasted Coco Flakes

Servings: 4

Prep Time: 8 minutes

Cooking Time: 10 minutes

Ingredients:

- 1 cup / 130 gr unsweetened coconut flakes
- ¼ / 50 gr cup granular erythritol.
- 2 tsp. / 10 ml coconut oil
- a pinch of salt

Directions:

1. Toss coconut flakes and oil in a large bowl until coated. Sprinkle with erythritol and salt. Place coconut flakes into the air fryer basket.
2. Adjust the temperature to 300 Degrees F / 150 °C and set the timer for 3 minutes.
3. Toss the flakes when 1 minute remains. Add an extra minute if you would like a more golden coconut flake.
4. You can store it in an airtight container for up to 3 days.

Nutritional Fact Per Serving: Calories: 165; Protein: 1.3g; Fibre: 2.7g; Fat: 15.5g; Carbs: 20.3g

108. Wine Infused Mushrooms

Servings: 3

Prep Time: 15 minutes

Cooking Time: 32 minutes

Ingredients

- ½ teaspoon garlic powder
- 1 tablespoon / 15 gr butter

- 2 pounds / 1 kg fresh mushrooms, quartered
- 2 tbsp. / 30 ml white vermouth
- 2 tsp. / 5 gr Herbs de Provence

Directions:

1. Set the temperature of the air fryer to 320 degrees F / 160°C.
2. Mix the butter, Herbs de Provence, and garlic powder in an air fryer pan and air fry for about 2 minutes.
3. Stir in the mushrooms and air fry for about 25 minutes.
4. Stir in the vermouth and air fry for 5 more minutes.
5. Remove from the air fryer and transfer the mushrooms onto serving plates. Serve hot.

Nutritional Fact Per Serving: Calories: 54 Carbohydrate: 5.3g Protein: 4.8g Fat: 2.4g Sugar: 2.7g Sodium: 23mg

109. Zucchini Mix and Herbed Eggplant

Servings: 3

Prep Time 10 minutes

Cooking Time:8 minutes

Ingredients:

- 1 eggplant
- 1 tsp of dried oregano
- 1 tsp of dried thyme
- 2 tbsp / 30 ml of lemon juice

- 3 cubed zucchinis
- 3 tbsp / 45 ml of olive oil
- Black pepper and salt

Directions:

1. Place the eggplants on the Air Fryer Grill Pan, and add thyme, zucchinis, olive oil, and salt.
2. Add pepper, oregano, and lemon juice.
3. Set the Air Fryer Grill to the air fry function.
4. Cook for 8 minutes at 360-degree F / 180°C
5. Serve immediately

Nutritional Fact Per Serving:

Calories: 55kcal, Fat: 1g, Carb: 13g, Proteins: 3g

SIDE DISH

110. Barley Risotto

Servings: 4

Prep time: 10 minutes

Cooking time: 30 minutes

Ingredients:

- ¾ pound / 350 gr barley
- 1 teaspoon of tarragon, dried
- 1 teaspoon of thyme, dried
- 2 garlic cloves, minced
- 2 ounces / 50 gr skim milk
- 2 pound / 1 kg sweet potato, peeled and chopped
- 2 yellow onions, chopped
- 3 ounces / 75 gr mushrooms, sliced
- 3 tbsp. / 45 ml olive oil
- 5 cups / 1,2 lt veggie stock
- Salt and black pepper to the taste

Directions:

1. Put stock in a pot, add barley, stir, bring to a boil over medium heat and cook for 15 minutes.
2. Heat your air fryer at 350 degrees F/180°C, add oil, and heat it. Add barley, onions, garlic, mushrooms, milk, salt, pepper, tarragon, and sweet potato,
3. Stir and cook for 15 minutes more.

4. Divide among plates and serve as a side dish.
5. Enjoy!

Nutritional Fact Per Serving: calories 124, fat 4, fiber 4, carbs 6, protein 4

111. Broccoli Mash

Servings: 4

Prep Time: 25 minutes

Cooking Time: 20-30 minutes

Ingredients:

- 20 oz. / 500 gr Broccoli florets
- 3 oz. / 75 gr Butter; melted
- 4 tbsp. / 5 gr Basil; chopped.
- A drizzle of olive oil
- A pinch of salt and black pepper
- One garlic clove; minced

Directions:

1. Take a bowl, mix the broccoli with the oil, salt, and pepper, and toss and transfer to your air fryer's basket.
2. Cook at 380°F / 190°C for 20 minutes, cool the broccoli down and put it in a blender
3. Add the rest of the ingredients, pulse, and divide the mash between plates
4. Serve as a side dish.

Nutritional Fact Per Serving: Calories: 200; Fat: 14g; Fibre: 3g; Carbs: 6g; Protein: 7g

112. CauliFlower Tots

Servings: 6

Prep Time: 15 minutes

Cooking Time: 10 minutes

Ingredients:

- 1 cup / 100 gr shredded cheddar
- ½ cup / 120 gr ketchup
- 2 tbsp. / 30 ml Sriracha
- 1 cup / 110 gr freshly grated Parmesan
- 1/3 cup / 60 gr readied rice
- 2/3 cup / 80 gr panko breadcrumbs
- Kosher salt
- 2 tbsp. / 1 bunch of freshly chopped chives
- Cooking spray
- 1 large egg, lightly beaten
- 4 cup / 500 gr cauliflower florets, steamed
- Freshly ground black pepper

Directions:

1. Process steamed cauliflower in a food processor till ready. Put the readied rice with cauliflower on a clean kitchen towel. Then squeeze to drain water.
2. Move cauliflower to a big bowl with panko, egg, cheddar, Parmesan, and chives. Now mix till combined. Season with pepper and salt as per the requirement.

3. One tablespoon mixture will be spooned and rolled into a tater-tot shape using your hands. Working in batches. These must be arranged in a single layer in the air fryer basket.
4. Then cook for 10 minutes at 375°F / 190°C or until tots turn golden.
5. Prepare spicy ketchup by combining ketchup and Sriracha in a small serving bowl. Stir well to mix.
6. Enjoy warm cauliflower tots along with spicy ketchup.

Nutritional Fact Per Serving: Calories: 200; Fat: 14g; Fibre: 3g; Carbs: 6g; Protein: 7g

113. Carrots and Rhubarb

Servings: 4

Prep time: 10 minutes

Cooking time: 40 minutes

Ingredients:

- ½ cup / 50 gr walnuts halved
- ½ teaspoon of stevia
- 1 orange, peeled, cut into medium segments, and zest grated
- 1 pound / 450 gr of baby carrots
- 1 pound/ 450 gr rhubarb, roughly chopped
- 2 tsp. / 10 ml walnut oil

Directions:

1. Put the oil in your air fryer, add carrots, toss and fry them at 380 degrees F / 190°C for 20 minutes.

2. Add rhubarb, orange zest, stevia, and walnuts, toss, and cook for 20 minutes more.
3. Add orange segments, toss and serve as a side dish.
4. Enjoy!

Nutritional Fact Per Serving: calories 172, fat 2, fiber 3, carbs 4, protein 4

114. Easy Polenta Pie

Servings: 3

Prep Time: 10 min

Cook time: 55 min

Ingredients:

- Chili beans, drained (15 ounces / 375 gr)
- Cornmeal (3/4 cup / 120 gr)
- Egg, slightly beaten (1 piece)
- Monterey Jack cheese, w/ jalapeno peppers, shredded (3/4 cup / 75 gr)
- Salt (a pinch)
- Tortilla chips/crushed corn (1/3 cup / 20 gr)
- Water (2 cups)

Directions:

1. Preheat your air fryer appliance to 350 degrees Fahrenheit / 180°C.
2. Mist cooking sprays onto a pie plate.
3. In a saucepan heated on medium-high, combine water, salt, and

cornmeal. Let the mixture boil, then cook on medium heat for six minutes. Stir in egg and let sit for five minutes.

4. Pour cornmeal mixture into pie plate and spread evenly. Air-fry for fifteen minutes and top with beans, corn chips, and cheese. Air-fry for another twenty minutes.

Nutritional Fact Per Serving: Calories 195 Fat 7.0 g Protein 10.0 g Carbohydrates 27.0 g

115. Garlic Beet Wedges

Servings: 4

Prep time: 10 minutes

Cooking time: 15 minutes

Ingredients:

- 4 beets, washed, peeled, and cut into large wedges
- 1 tablespoon / 15 ml olive oil
- Salt and black to the taste
- 2 garlic cloves, minced
- 1 teaspoon / 5 ml lemon juice

Directions:

1. Mix beets with oil, salt, pepper, garlic, and lemon juice in a bowl.
2. Transfer to your air fryer's basket and cook them at 400 degrees F / 200°C for 15 minutes.
3. Divide beets wedges between plates and serve as a side dish.
4. Enjoy!

Rachel Vitale

Air Fryer Cookbook for Beginners

Nutritional Fact Per Serving: calories 182, fat 6, fiber 3, carbs 8, protein 2

116. Honey Butternut Mix

Servings: 4

Prep time: 10 minutes

Cooking time: 20 minutes

Ingredients:

- ½ teaspoon of allspice, ground
- ½ teaspoon of nutmeg, ground
- 1 pound / 450 gr butternut squash, peeled and cut into medium chunks
- 1 tablespoon / 15 ml avocado oil
- 2 tbsp. / 30 gr butter, melted
- 2 tbsp. / 40 gr honey
- Salt and black pepper to the taste

Directions:

1. Mix the squash with the melted butter, nutmeg, and other ingredients in a pan that fits your air fryer.
2. Introduce in the fryer and cook at 370 degrees F / 190°C for 20 minutes.
3. Divide the mix between plates and serve as a side dish.

Nutritional Fact Per Serving: calories 200, fat 6, fiber 7, carbs 15, protein 5

117. Hasselback Potatoes

Servings: 4

Prep Time: 20 minutes

Cooking Time: 30 minutes

Ingredients

- 1 tablespoon / 1 bunch of fresh chives, chopped
- 2 tbsp. / 30 ml olive oil
- 2 tbsp. / 15 gr Parmesan cheese, shredded
- 4 potatoes

Directions:

1. With a sharp knife, cut slits along with each potato the short way, about ¼-inch apart, making sure slices should stay connected at the bottom.
2. Set the temp of your air fryer to 355 degrees F / 180°C. Grease an air fryer basket. Gently brush each potato evenly with oil.
3. Arrange potatoes into the prepared air fryer basket. Air fry for about 30 minutes, coating with the oil once halfway through.
4. Remove from the air fryer and transfer the potatoes onto a platter.
5. Garnish with the cheeses and chives and serve immediately.

Nutritional Fact Per Serving: Calories: 218 Carbohydrate: 33.6g Protein: 4.6g Fat: 7.9g Sugar: 2.5g Sodium: 55mg

118. Kale and Cauliflower Mash

Servings: 4

Prep Time: 25 minutes

Cooking Time: 20-30 minutes

Ingredients:

- 1 cauliflower head, florets separated
- 1 tbsp. / 1 bunch of Parsley; chopped.
- 1/3 cup / 80 gr coconut cream
- 2 scallions; chopped.
- 3 cups kale; chopped.
- 4 garlic cloves; minced
- 4 tsp. / 20 gr Butter; melted
- A pinch of salt and black pepper

Directions:

1. In a pan that fits the air fryer, combine the cauliflower with the butter, garlic, scallions, salt, pepper, and the cream, and toss to mix properly.
2. Introduce the pan into the machine and cook at 380°F / 190°C for 20 minutes
3. Mash the mix well, add the remaining ingredients, and whisk together.
4. Divide between plates and serve.

Nutritional Fact Per Serving: Calories: 198; Fat: 9g; Fibre: 2g; Carbs: 6g; Protein: 8g

119. Mango and Cherry Rice

Servings: 4

Prep time: 10 minutes

Cooking time: 20 minutes

Ingredients:

- 1 cup / 90 gr wild rice
- ½ cup / 60 gr mango, peeled and cubed
- ¼ cup / 35 gr cup cherries pitted and halved
- 1 tablespoon / 15 ml avocado oil
- ½ teaspoon of sweet paprika
- Salt and black pepper to the taste
- 1 tablespoon / 1 bunch of chives, chopped

Directions:

1. In a pan that fits your air fryer, mix the rice with the mango, cherries, with the other ingredients, and toss together.
2. Introduce the air fryer and cook at 370 degrees F / 190°C for 20 minutes.
3. Divide between plates and serve as a side dish.

Nutritional Fact Per Serving: calories 200, fat 4, fiber 5, carbs 11, protein 4

120. Mozzarella Corn and Peppers Mix

Servings: 4

Prep time: 5 minutes

Cooking time: 20 minutes

Ingredients:

- 1 cup / 170 gr corn
- 1 cup / 120 gr mozzarella, shredded
- 1 tablespoon / 4 gr cilantro, chopped
- 1 tablespoon / 15 ml olive oil
- 1-pound / 450 gr red bell peppers, cut into strips
- Juice of 1 lime
- Salt and black pepper to the taste

Directions:

1. In the air fryer's pan, mix the peppers with the corn and the other ingredients except for the cheese and toss.
2. Sprinkle the cheese on top, introduce the dish to the air fryer and cook at 370 degrees F / 190°C for 20 minutes.
3. Divide the mix between plates and serve as a side dish.

Nutritional Fact Per Serving: calories 200, fat 8, fiber 2, carbs 5, protein 8

121. Mushrooms and Sour Cream

Servings: 3

Prep time: 10 minutes

Cooking time: 10 minutes

Ingredients:

- 2 bacon strips, chopped
- 1 yellow onion, chopped
- 1 green bell pepper, chopped
- 24 mushrooms, stems removed
- 1 carrot, grated
- ½ cup / 120 gr sour cream
- 1 cup / 100 gr cheddar cheese, grated
- Salt and black pepper to the taste

Directions:

1. Heat a pan over medium-high heat, add bacon, onion, bell pepper, and carrot, stir and cook for 1 minute.
2. Add salt, pepper, and sour cream, stir, cook for 1 minute more, take off the heat and cool down.
3. Stuff mushrooms with this mix, sprinkle cheese on top, and cook at 360 degrees F / 180°C for 8 minutes.
4. Divide among plates and serve as a side dish. Enjoy!

Nutritional Fact Per Serving: Calories 213, fat 4, fiber 8, carbs 8, protein 3

122. Onion Rings Side Dish

Servings: 3

Prep time: 10 minutes

Cooking time: 10 minutes

Ingredients:

- ¾ cup / 90 gr bread crumbs
- 1 ¼ / 190 gr cups white flour
- 1 cup / 240 ml milk
- 1 onion cut into medium slices and rings separated
- 1 teaspoon of baking powder
- A pinch of salt
- 1 egg

Directions:

1. Mix flour with salt and baking powder in a bowl, stir, dredge onion rings in this mix, and place them on a separate plate.
2. Add milk and egg to the flour mix and whisk well.
3. Dip onion rings in this mix, dredge them in breadcrumbs, put them in your air fryer's basket, and cook them at 360 degrees F / 170°C for 10 minutes.
4. Divide among plates and serve as a side dish for a steak. Enjoy!

Nutritional Fact Per Serving: calories 140, fat 8, fiber 20, carbs 12, protein 3

123. Pumpkin Rice

Servings: 4

Prep time: 5 minutes

Cooking time: 30 minutes

Ingredients:

- 2 tbsp. / 30 ml olive oil
- 1 small yellow onion, chopped
- 2 garlic cloves, minced
- 12 ounces / 300 gr white rice
- 4 cups / 1 lt chicken stock
- 6 ounces / 150 gr pumpkin puree
- ½ teaspoon of nutmeg
- 1 teaspoon of thyme, chopped
- ½ teaspoon of ginger, grated
- ½ teaspoon of cinnamon powder
- ½ teaspoon of allspice
- 4 ounces / 100 gr heavy cream

Directions:

1. In a dish that fits your air fryer, mix oil with onion, garlic, rice, stock, pumpkin puree, nutmeg, thyme, ginger, cinnamon, allspice, and cream; stir well.
2. Place in your air fryer's basket and cook at 360 degrees F / 180 °C for 30 minutes.
3. Divide among plates and serve as a side dish.
4. Enjoy!

Nutritional Fact Per Serving: calories 261, fat 6, fiber 7, carbs 29, protein 4

124. Squash Casserole

Servings: 3

Prep Time: 20 min

Cooking time: 40 min

Ingredients:

- Brown rice, cooked (1 cup / 190 gr)
- Italian cheese blend, gluten-free, shredded (1/2 cup / 50 gr)
- Olive oil, extra virgin (1 tablespoon / 15 ml)
- Onion, diced (1/2 cup / 25 gr)
- Pepper (a pinch)
- Plum tomato, diced (1 piece)
- Salt (1/2 teaspoon)
- Thyme leaves, fresh, chopped (1 tablespoon / 1 bunch)
- Yellow summer squash, medium, sliced thinly (1 piece)
- Zucchini, medium, sliced thinly (1 piece)

Directions:

1. Preheat the air fryer to 375 degrees Fahrenheit / 190°C.
2. Mist cooking sprays onto a gratin dish.
3. Combine rice, onion, tomato, pepper, salt (1/4 teaspoon / a pinch), oil, and ½ thyme leaves. Spread evenly into a gratin dish and layer on top with squash and zucchini. Sprinkle with remaining salt (1/4 teaspoon/ a pinch) and thyme.
4. Cover and air-fry for twenty minutes. Top with cheese and air-fry for another ten to twelve minutes.

Nutritional Fact Per Serving: Calories 110 Fat 5.0 g Protein 4.0 g Carbohydrates 12.0 g

DESSERTS

125. Apple Crumble

servings: 4

Prep Time: 10 minutes

Cooking Time: 25 minutes

Ingredients

- ¼ cup / 60 gr butter softened
- 1 (14-ounces / 350gr) can of apple pie filling
- 7 tbsp. / 100 gr caster sugar
- 9 tbsp. / 100 gr self-rising flour
- A pinch of salt

Directions:

1. Set the temperature of the air fryer to 320 degrees F / 160°C. Lightly grease a baking dish.
2. Place apple pie filling evenly into the prepared baking dish.
3. In a medium bowl, add the remaining ingredients and mix until a crumbly mixture forms.
4. Spread the mixture evenly over the apple pie filling. Arrange the baking dish in an air fryer basket. Air fry for about 25 minutes.
5. Remove the baking dish from the air fryer and place it onto a wire rack to cool for about 10 minutes. Serve warm.

Nutritional Fact Per Serving: Calories: 340 Carbohydrate: 60.3g Protein: 2g Fat: 11.8g Sugar: 34.8g Sodium: 167mg

Nutritional Fact Per Serving: Calories: 205 Carbohydrate: 30.3g Protein: 3.2g Fat: 8.9g Sugar: 14.4g Sodium: 96mg

126. Banana Choco Pastries

Servings: 4

Prep Time: 15 minutes

Cooking Time: 12 minutes

Ingredients

- ½ cup / 140 gr Nutella
- 1 puff pastry sheet
- 2 bananas, peeled and sliced

Directions:

1. Cut the pastry sheet into 4 equal-sized squares. Spread Nutella evenly on each square of pastry.
2. Divide the banana slices over Nutella. Fold each square into a triangle and slightly press the edges with wet fingers.
3. Then with a fork, press the edges firmly.
4. Set the temp of your air fryer to 375 degrees F / 190°C. Lightly grease an air fryer basket.
5. Arrange pastries into the prepared air fryer basket in a single layer. Air fry for about 10-12 minutes.
6. Remove from the air fryer and transfer the pastries onto a platter. Serve warm.

127. Bread Pudding

Servings: 4

Prep Time: 15 minutes

Cooking Time: 15 minutes

Ingredients

- 2 oz. / 50 gr semisweet chocolate
- 4 slices day-old bread
- ½ cup / 100 gr sugar
- ½ cup / 120 gr 2% milk
- ½ cup / 120 gr half-and-half cream
- 1 egg
- 1 teaspoon of vanilla extract
- 1 pinch of salt

Directions:

1. In a microwave-safe bowl, melt chocolate; stir until smooth. Stir in cream; set aside.
2. Whisk sugar, milk, egg, vanilla, and salt in a bowl. Stir in the chocolate mixture.
3. Add bread cubes without crusts and toss to coat. Let stand for 10 minutes.
4. Preheat the air fryer to 325°F / 160°C.
5. Spoon bread mixture into 2 greased 8-oz. ramekins (200 gr).
6. Place on a tray in the air-fryer basket and cook for 15 minutes.

Nutritional Fact Per Serving: Calories: 470 Carbs: 30.3g Protein: 3.2g Fat: 8.9g

128. Butter Cake

Servings: 9

Prep Time: 30 minutes

Cooking Time: 15 minutes

Ingredients

- Cooking spray
- ¼ cup / 50gr white sugar
- 7 tbsp. / 100 gr butter, at room temperature
- 2 tbsp. / 25 gr white sugar
- 1 egg
- 1 tablespoon / 15 gr salt, or to taste
- ½ cup / 80 gr all-purpose flour
- 6 tbsp. / 100 ml milk

Directions:

1. Preheat your air fryer to 350°F (180°C). Using cooking spray, coat a small fluted tube pan.
2. In a large bowl, beat the butter and 1/4 cup plus 2 tbsp. of sugar with an electric mixer until light and fluffy. Mix in the egg until it is smooth and frothy.
3. Combine flour and salt in a mixing bowl. Add the milk and completely combine the batter. Transfer the batter to the prepared pan and smooth the top with the back of a spoon.
4. In the air fryer basket, place the pan. Make a 15-minute timer on your clock. Cook until a toothpick put into the center of the cake comes out clean.
5. Remove the cake from the pan and set it aside to cool for 5 minutes.

Nutritional Fact Per Serving: Calories: 470 Carbs: 30.3g Protein: 3.2g Fat: 8.9g

129. Clafoutis

servings: 4

Prep Time: 15 minutes

Cooking Time: 25 minutes

Ingredients

- ¼ cup / 40 gr flour
- ¼ cup / 30 gr powdered sugar
- ½ cup / 120 gr sour cream
- 1 egg
- 1 tablespoon / 15 gr butter
- 1½ cups / 200 gr fresh cherries pitted
- 2 tbsp. / 30 gr sugar
- 3 tbsp. / 45 ml vodka
- Pinch of salt

Directions:

1. Mix the cherries and vodka ingredients together in a bowl.
2. Mix flour, sugar, and salt in a separate basin. Mix in the sour cream and egg until a smooth dough is achieved.

3. Heat the food in the air fryer to a temperature of 355°F / 180 °C. Add butter to a cake pan.
4. Fill the cake pan two-thirds full of the flour mixture. Cover the dough with the cherry mixture. Place dots of butter on top.
5. Arrange the cake pan in an air fryer basket. Air fry for about 25 minutes or until a toothpick inserted in the center comes clean.
6. Remove the cake pan from the air fryer and place it onto a wire rack to cool for about 10 minutes.
7. Now, invert the Clafoutis onto a platter and sprinkle with powdered sugar.
8. Cut the Clafoutis into desired size slices and serve warm.

Nutritional Fact Per Serving: Calories: 226 Carbohydrate: 25.5g Protein: 3.5g Fat: 10.2g Sugar: 0.8g Sodium: 191g

130. Choco Cream Cake

Servings: 3

Prep Time: 15 minutes

Cooking Time: 25 minutes

Ingredients

- 1 cup / 150 gr flour
- 1 teaspoon of baking powder
- ½ teaspoon of baking soda
- 3 eggs
- ½ cup / 120 gr sour cream
- ½ cup / 100 gr butter softened
- 2 tsp. / a pinch of vanilla extract
- 1/3 cup / 30 gr cocoa powder
- a pinch of salt
- 2/3 cup / 150 gr sugar

Directions:

1. Mix flour, cocoa powder, baking powder, baking powder, baking soda, and salt in a large bowl.
2. Add the remaining ingredients and with an electric whisker, whisk on low speed until well combined.
3. Set the temperature of the air fryer to 320 degrees F / 160°C. Lightly grease a cake pan. Place mixture evenly into the prepared cake pan.
4. Arrange the cake pan into an air fryer basket. Air fry for about 25 minutes or until a toothpick inserted in the center comes clean.
5. Remove the cake pan from the air fryer and place it onto a wire rack to cool for about 10 minutes.
6. Now, invert the cake onto a wire rack to completely cool before slicing. Cut the cake into desired size slices and serve.

Nutritional Fact Per Serving: Calories: 383 Carbohydrate: 42.3g Protein: 6.6g Fat: 22.4g Sugar: 22.8g Sodium: 307mg

131. Chocolate Banana Pastries

servings: 4

Prep Time: 15 minutes

Cooking Time: 12 minutes

Ingredients

- ½ cup / 140 gr Nutella
- 1 puff pastry sheet
- 2 bananas, peeled and sliced

Directions:

1. Cut the pastry sheet into 4 equal-sized squares. Spread Nutella evenly on each square of pastry.
2. Divide the banana slices over Nutella. Fold each square into a triangle and slightly press the edges with wet fingers.
3. Then with a fork, press the edges firmly.
4. Set the temp of your air fryer to 375 degrees F. Lightly grease an air fryer basket.
5. Arrange pastries into the prepared air fryer basket in a single layer. Air fry for about 10-12 minutes.
6. Remove from the air fryer and transfer the pastries onto a platter. Serve warm.

Nutritional Fact Per Serving: Calories: 205 Carbohydrate: 30.3g Protein: 3.2g Fat: 8.9g Sugar: 14.4g Sodium: 96mg

132. Cocoa Brownies

servings: 2

Prep Time: 15 minutes

Cooking Time: 18 minutes

Ingredients

- ½ cup / 110 gr granulated sugar
- ¼ cup / 40 gr all-purpose flour
- 1/3 cup / 30 gr cocoa powder
- A pinch of kosher salt
- 1 large egg
- a pinch of baking powder
- ¼ cup / 60 gr melted butter, cooled slightly

Directions:

1. Using cooking spray, grease a 6 inches round cake pan. Mix sugar, cocoa powder, flour, baking powder, and salt in a medium bowl.
2. Whisk egg and melted butter in a small bowl until well mixed. Stir together the wet and dry ingredients until everything is well blended.
3. Smooth the top of the brownie batter into the prepared cake pan. Cook for 16–18 minutes in an air fryer at 350°F / 180°C.
4. Allow 10 minutes to cool before slicing.

Nutritional Fact Per Serving: Calories: 114 Carbs: 30.3g Protein: 3.2g Fat: 8.9g

133. Doughnuts Pudding

Servings: 4

Prep Time: 15 minutes

Cooking Time: 60 minutes

Ingredients

- ¼ cup / 50 gr sugar
- ½ cup / 75 gr raisins
- ½ cup / 75 gr semi-sweet chocolate baking chips
- ¾ cup / 100 gr frozen sweet cherries
- 1 teaspoon of ground cinnamon
- 1 ½ cup / 180 gr whipping cream
- 4 egg yolks
- 6 glazed doughnuts, cut into small pieces

Directions:

1. Mix doughnut pieces, cherries, raisins, chocolate chips, sugar, and cinnamon in a large bowl.
2. Whisk the egg yolks and heavy cream in a separate dish until thoroughly mixed.
3. Add the egg yolk mix into the doughnut mixture and mix well.
4. Set the temperature of the air fryer to 310 degrees F / 150 °C. Line a baking dish with a piece of foil.
5. Place the doughnut mixture evenly into the prepared baking dish.
6. Arrange the baking dish into an air fryer basket. Air fry for about 60 minutes.
7. Remove from the air fryer and serve warm.

Nutritional Fact Per Serving: Calories: 786 Carbohydrate: 9.3g Protein: 11g Fat: 43.2g Sugar: 60.7g Sodium: 419mg

134. Easy Plantain Cupcakes

Servings 4

Prep Time: 5 minutes

Cooking Time: 10 minutes

Ingredients

- 1 cup / 150 gr all-purpose flour
- 1 egg, whisked
- 1 teaspoon of baking powder
- 1/4 cup / 45 gr brown sugar
- a pinch of ground cinnamon
- a pinch of ground cloves
- 2 ripe plantains, peeled and mashed with a fork
- 2 tbsp. / 20 gr raisins, soaked
- 4 tbsp. / 60 ml coconut oil, room temperature
- 4 tbsp. / 30 gr pecans, roughly chopped
- A pinch of salt

Directions

1. In a mixing bowl, thoroughly combine all ingredients until everything is well incorporated.

2. Spoon the batter into a greased muffin tin.
3. Bake the plantain cupcakes in your Air Fryer at 350 degrees F / 180 °C for about 10 minutes or until golden brown on the top.
4. Bon appétit!

Nutritional Fact Per Serving: Calories 471; Fat 22.5g; Carbs 65.8g; Protein 6.9g; Sugars 24.2g

135. Figs and Grapes Bowls

Servings: 4

Prep time: 10 minutes

Cooking time: 15 minutes

Ingredients:

- ½ teaspoon of nutmeg powder
- 1 cup / 230 gr heavy cream
- 2 cups / 600 gr figs, halved
- 2 cups / 320 gr red grapes
- 2 tbsp. / 25 gr sugar

Directions:

1. In your air fryer's pan, combine the figs with the grapes and other ingredients, and toss them together.
2. Cook at 360 degrees F / 180°C for 15 minutes.
3. Divide into bowls and serve.

Nutritional Fact Per Serving: calories 180, fat 6, fiber 8, carbs 19, protein 12

136. Fruity Crumble

Servings: 4

Prep Time: 15 minutes

Cooking Time: 20 minutes

Ingredients

- ¼ cup / 60 gr chilled butter, cubed
- ½ pound / 220 gr fresh apricots pitted and cubed
- 1 cup / 130 gr fresh blackberries
- 1 tablespoon / 15 ml cold water
- 1 tablespoon / 15 ml fresh lemon juice
- 1/3 cup sugar / 75 gr, divided
- 7/8 cup / 130 gr flour
- Pinch of salt

Directions:

1. 390 degrees Fahrenheit / 200°C is a good starting point for the air fryer. Bake a cake in a pan that has been coated with cooking spray.
2. Combine the apricots, blackberries, sugar, and lemon juice in a large bowl. Place the apricot mixture in the baking dish that has been previously prepared.
3. Add the remaining sugar, salt, water, and butter to a second dish and mix it together. Mix until a crumbly mixture forms. Spread the flour mixture evenly over the apricot mixture.

4. Place the pan in an air fryer basket. Air fry for about 20 minutes.
5. Remove the baking pan from the air fryer and place it onto a wire rack to cool for about 10 minutes. Serve warm.

Nutritional Fact Per Serving: Calories: 307 Carbohydrate: 47.3g Protein: 4.2g Fat: 12.4g Sugar: 23.7g Sodium: 123mg

137. Grapes and Rhubarb Mix

Servings: 4

Prep time: 10 minutes

Cooking time: 15 minutes

Ingredients:

- 1-pound / 450 gr red grapes
- 1 ½ cups / 300 gr rhubarb, sliced
- 1 cup / 240 ml apple juice
- 1 cup / 240 ml grape juice
- 3 tbsp. / 40 gr sugar
- Juice and zest of 1 lime

Directions:

1. Mix the grapes with the rhubarb and other ingredients in a pan that fits your air fryer.
2. Introduce in the fryer and cook at 350 degrees F / 180°C for 15 minutes.
3. Divide into bowls and serve cold.

Nutritional Fact Per Serving: calories 151, fat 4, fiber 5, carbs 8, protein 4

138. Maple Chia Bowls

Servings: 4

Prep time: 10 minutes

Cooking time: 20 minutes

Ingredients:

- ½ cup / 80 gr raisins
- 1 cup / 240 ml almond milk
- 1 tablespoon / 15 gr maple syrup
- a pinch vanilla extract
- 2 tbsp. / 30 ml sugar
- 4 tbsp. / 40 gr chia seeds

Directions:

1. Mix the chia seeds with the maple syrup and the other ingredients in a pan that fits your air fryer.
2. Introduce in the fryer and cook at 360 degrees F / 180°C for 20 minutes.
3. Divide into bowls and serve cold.

Nutritional Fact Per Serving: calories 161, fat 5, fiber 4, carbs 16, protein 5

139. Homemade Chelsea Currant Buns

Servings 4

Prep time: 20 minutes

Cooking time: 30 minutes

Ingredients

- 1 egg, whisked
- 1-ounce / 25 gr icing sugar
- a pinch of dry yeast
- 1/2 cup / 75 gr dried currants
- 1/2 cup /p 120 ml milk, warm
- 1/2-pound / 220 gr cake flour
- 2 tbsp. / 30 gr granulated sugar
- 4 tablespoon / 60 grs butter
- A pinch of sea salt

Directions

1. Mix the flour, yeast, sugar, and salt in a bowl; add milk, egg, and 2 tbsp. of butter and combine well. Add lukewarm water as necessary to form a smooth dough.
2. Knead the dough until it is elastic; then, leave it in a warm place to rise for 30 minutes.
3. Roll out your dough and spread the remaining 2 tbsp. of butter onto the dough; scatter dried currants over the dough.
4. Cut into 8 equal slices and roll them up. Brush each bun with non-stick cooking oil and transfer them to the Air Fryer cooking basket.
5. Cook your buns at 330 degrees F / 160°C for about 20 minutes, turning them over halfway through the cooking time.
6. Dust with icing sugar before serving. Bon appétit!

Nutritional Fact Per Serving: Calories 395; Fat 14g; Carbs 56.1g; Protein 7.6g; Sugars 13.6g

140. Plums, Avocado and Grapes Stew

Servings: 4

Prep time: 10 minutes

Cooking time: 20 minutes

Ingredients:

- 1 cup /150 gr avocado, peeled, pitted, and cubed
- 1 cup / 170 gr plums, pitted and halved
- 1 cup / 160 gr red grapes
- 1 cup / 240 ml water
- 2 tbsp. / 30 ml lime juice
- 2 tbsp. / 30 gr sugar

Directions:

1. In a pan that fits your air fryer, mix the plums with the grapes plus the other ingredients, and stir.
2. Introduce in the fryer and cook at 330 degrees F / 160°C for 20 minutes.

3. Divide the mix into bowls and serve cold.

Nutritional Fact Per Serving: calories 171, fat 1, fiber 3, carbs 16, protein 6

141. Raisin Bread Pudding

Servings: 3

Prep Time: 15 minutes

Cooking Time: 12 minutes

Ingredients

- A pinch of vanilla extract
- ½ teaspoon of ground cinnamon
- 1 cup / 240 ml milk
- 1 egg
- 1 tablespoon / 10 gr brown sugar
- 1 tablespoon / 10 gr chocolate chips
- 1 tablespoon / 15 gr sugar
- 2 bread slices, cut into small cubes
- 2 tbsp. / 30 gr raisins, soaked in hot water for about 15 minutes

Directions:

1. Mix milk, egg, brown sugar, cinnamon, and vanilla extract well in a bowl. Stir in the raisins.
2. In a baking dish, spread the bread cubes and top evenly with the milk mixture. Refrigerate for about 15-20 minutes.
3. Set the temperature of your air fryer to 375 degrees F / 190°C.
4. Remove from refrigerator and sprinkle with chocolate chips and sugar on top.
5. Arrange the baking dish into an air fryer basket. Air fry for about 12 minutes.
6. Remove from the air fryer and serve warm.

Nutritional Fact Per Serving: Calories: 143 Carbohydrate: 21.3g Protein: 5.5g Fat: 4.4g Sugar: 16.4g Sodium: 104mg

142. Tasty Shortbread Cookies

Servings: 4

Prep Time: 25 min

Cooking time: 1 hr 5 min

Ingredients:

- Powdered sugar (3/4 cup / 80 gr)
- Flour, all-purpose (2 ½ cups / 375 gr)
- Butter softened (1 cup / 220 gr)
- Vanilla (a pinch)

Directions:

1. Preheat the air fryer to 325 degrees Fahrenheit / 160°C.
2. Combine butter, vanilla, and powdered sugar with flour to form a soft dough.
3. Roll out dough and cut out 4 circles. Place on a cookie sheet.

4. Air-fry for fourteen to sixteen minutes.

Nutritional Fact Per Serving: Calories 70 Fat 4.0 g Protein 0 g Carbohydrates 7.0 g

Nutritional Fact Per Serving:

Calories: 182; Fat: 12g; Fibre: 1g; Carbs: 3g; Protein: 6g

143. Walnut and Vanilla Bars

Servings: 4

Prep Time: 21 minutes

Cooking time: 16 minutes

Ingredients:

- ¼ cup / 30 gr almond flour
- ¼ cup/ 30 gr walnuts; chopped.
- ½ tsp. of baking soda
- 1 egg
- 1 tsp. of vanilla extract
- 1/3 cup / 30 gr cocoa powder
- 3 tbsp. / 20 gr swerve
- 7 tbsp. 100 gr ghee; melted

Directions:

1. Take a bowl and mix all the ingredients and stir well.
2. Spread this on a baking sheet that fits your air fryer lined with parchment paper.
3. Put it in the fryer and cook at 330°F / 160°C and bake for 16 minutes
4. Leave the bars to cool down, cut and serve

REFERENCES

Cheyenne Lentz (April 1, 2019). "7 things you should cook in an air fryer and 7 things you shouldn't". Insider. Retrieved June 15, 2020.

Melinda Cuzo (May 1, 2020). "The Features of an Air Fryer". Aifryer.net. Retrieved June 20, 2020.

Laurel Randolph (Feb 23, 2022). "A guide to converting any oven, stovetop, or deep-fryer recipe for your air fryer". Insider. Retrieved June 19, 2020.

Printed in Great Britain
by Amazon

85648226R00061